SAMS Monograph Series

Population-Centric Counterinsurgency: A False Idol?

Three Monographs from the School of Advanced Military Studies

Edited and Introduced by
Dan G. Cox and Thomas Bruscino
AY 10-01

Cover Photo Credit: US Army
Specialist Carlos R. Hansen and fellow Soldiers of the personal security detachment for
Headquarters and Headquarters Troop, 1st Squadron, 113th Cavalry Regiment, Task Force
Redhorse, patrol the villages in the Bagram Security Zone.

Published by Books Express Publishing
Copyright © Books Express, 2012
ISBN 978-1-78039-804-4

Books Express publications are available from all good retail and online booksellers. For
publishing proposals and direct ordering please contact us at: info@books-express.com

Contents

Contents

Introduction

Dan G. Cox and Thomas Bruscino

Rarely is it a good idea for any field of human endeavor to be dominated by a single theory aimed at addressing a pressing problem. However, such dominance has recently occurred in the American approach to counterinsurgency warfare. In recent years, driven by the perceived failures in the American war in Iraq, the United States military, and in particular the United States Army, has determined that when it comes to counterinsurgency, the population-centric approach is the only way to go. The population-centric approach dominates the Army's capstone manual on Counterinsurgency, Field Manual 3-24, a document published in late 2006 in order to help redress shortcomings in fighting the war in Iraq.[1]

The driving force behind the manual, General David Petraeus, took the principles contained therein with him to Iraq, applied them during the famous surge of 2007-2008, and ultimately turned that war around. According to this popular account, the population-centric approach had been vindicated, and it became something of received truth about how to prosecute counterinsurgency.

The Origins and Implications of Population-Centric Counterinsurgency

On its face, this would not seem to be much of a problem. In its broad outlines, there is little that is objectionable to the population-centric approach as it is written in FM 3-24. The manual itself does not state that violent force is unnecessary; rather it calls for balance in the use of force in any counterinsurgency effort, depending on the situation itself. Certainly the general population must receive much of the time and consideration of the counterinsurgent force. If that was all there was to the population-centric approach that dominates the field today, few would have any problems with it.

However, the current population-centric approach is something more than even the sum of the parts of FM 3-24. The manual emerged from and exists within a much larger intellectual environment, and that environment rounds out the full meaning and intended implications of its contents. A relatively small but influential group of military theorists and students of military affairs, driven by varying motivations, have had a large effect on the meaning of the population-centric approach.

First, it is impossible to understand the current population-centric approach without accounting for the importance of the Vietnam War. Almost immediately after the conflict ended, certain critics of the war made a strong argument that military deserved the lion's share of the blame for the loss. Led by Andrew Krepinevich, such critics argued that the Americans erroneously fought with a solely conventional emphasis that deliberately overlooked the counterinsurgency side of the war.[2] More recent commentators like David Ucko use the Vietnam experience to hammer home the argument that the U. S. Army is "uncomfortable" with counterinsurgency operations and has always had a severe bias toward conventional warfare. These and numerous other critics argue that the U. S. Army has a predilection toward conventional warfighting because it is easier.[3] Some recent works have emphasized that the military did turn its attention to counterinsurgency after 1968 and achieved great military successes, but even these works have been used to drive home the argument that the military switched too late because of its traditional aversion to counterinsurgency.[4]

Such arguments have not gone unanswered, and indeed for years other students of Vietnam made equally impassioned cases that failure of the war came from poor political guidance and strategic choices.[5] Others have even made the case that American military leaders did the best with the situation they had, considering they had to contend simultaneously with conventional and insurgent threats.[6] Nevertheless, when the war in Iraq seemed to be a lost cause, the traditional arguments about the military's failings at counterinsurgency in Vietnam gained traction. It became conventional wisdom that if only the U.S. military would spend more time and effort on counterinsurgency that they would not struggle so mightily every time they became involved in such small wars. The writing and dissemination of FM 3-24 would be a central component of the effort to fix that historical problem.

But there had to be more to the effort than just spending time on counterinsurgency. Part of the promise of the critics of the military's historical conventional-focused approach was that they knew what kind of counterinsurgency would have won the war. In order to be consistent, their kind of counterinsurgency had to be as far as possible from the conventional warfare that they had so vehemently critiqued. Since so much of conventional warfare is built around the overwhelmingly application of violence, violence itself became implicit and sometimes explicit stand-in for the wrong way of fighting.

If not violence, then what? The newly ascendant counterinsurgency advocates turned to historical theory. The roots of their thinking can be found in a selective reading of the seminal counterinsurgency works by Mao, David Galula, Robert Thompson, and Frank Kitson. Among these, Galula took on a certain degree of primacy in military education on counterinsurgency, as became evident when General David Petraeus purchased roughly 1,500 copies of *Counterinsurgency Warfare* as the Combined Arms Center commandant and directed that every major going through the Command and General Staff College be assigned this reading. While there is much that can be gleaned from Galula's work, population-centric proponents have focused on the disadvantages counterinsurgents face when employing violence. In fact, Galula argues that "A soldier fired upon in conventional war who does not fire back with every available weapon would be guilty of a dereliction of his duty; the reverse would be the case in counterinsurgency warfare, where the rule is to apply a minimum of fire."[7] The key instead, according to the British theorists like Thompson and Kitson, is to win the "hearts and minds" of the population. Such efforts are best done through non-violent and non-coercive means, and thus aid and development became a major component of counterinsurgency.

Contemporary interpreters of such theory, including some of the driving forces behind FM 3-24, have said as much. For example, John Nagl has been one of the most vociferous proponents of population-centric counterinsurgency. Nagl argues that "protecting the population was the key to success in any counterinsurgency campaign" and, like Galula, Nagl further posits that this means that the Army has to shift away from its overreliance on firepower to win wars.[8] Lieutenant Colonel Robert M. Cassidy adds that population-centric counterinsurgency must focus on denying the insurgent safe haven but again the counterinsurgent should attempt to fight alongside indigenous forces and when possible allow indigenous forces to lead.[9] Cassidy adds lessons he feels come from the U.S. Indian wars of "a close civil military coordination of the pacification effort," "fair paternalistic governance," and reformation of the "economic and educational spheres," to the list of tasks a population-centric counterinsurgent should complete.[10] Heather Gregg makes this point more sharply arguing that successful counterinsurgency can only be achieved through "population engagement, stability operations, and the creation of a functional state."[11] These tenets really amount to the modern day notion of nation-building and they dovetail nicely into the non-kinetic emphasis of population-centric counterinsurgency.[12] Other implications from this thinking are that a large ground force contingent will be necessary and that the counterinsurgency will take many years to successfully complete.[13]

While the population-centric approach is dominant currently, it does have its complications. For example, Colonel Gian Gentile has made the case that the population-centric proponents have reduced counterinsurgency to a "strategy of tactics" thus obviating both the operational and strategic aspects of counterinsurgency.[14] Population-centric proponents often fail to mention that Galula clearly identifies two key points in an insurgency when kinetic force will work. One point, as argued by Galula, Kitson, and modern counterinsurgency theorist Bard O'Neill, is early in the insurgency formation stages when mobilization is just beginning.[15] Of perhaps even greater interest is Galula's assertion that there is a second opportunity for the counterinsurgent to use military force to destroy an insurgency. Galula argues that the insurgent cannot remain clandestine engaging only in harassing attacks and terrorism indefinitely. Instead, the successful insurgent must eventually switch over to a conventional force and defeat the national government through conventional means. The point when the insurgent begins to switch to a conventional approach is a tenuous one. If this point is successfully identified, then the counterinsurgent can attack and destroy the insurgency in one fell swoop.[16]

Regardless of these concerns and the way many theorists directly contradict the implied and explicit violence aversion of the current population-centric approach, the current view has taken hold as *the* answer.

Learning How to Think About Counterinsurgency

Perhaps one of the key problems with the study of warfare is that there has been little acknowledgement that warfare is a social science endeavor. Despite there being famous and oft-quoted theoretical works on warfare, there is no coherent academic field devoted to studying warfare as there is dedicated to the study of politics or history.[17] The problem is especially acute in the field of counterinsurgency. For while Paul David Reynolds argues that any social science theory must be rigorously formulated, examined, and most importantly, be based on empirical evidence and inquiry,[18] such standards were not met before population-centric counterinsurgency was anointed as *the* answer to insurgency.[19] The consensus occurred with no empirical inquiry and little historical reference seemingly through an accident of historical timing and the force of a few charismatic and influential personalities.

It is worthwhile, then, to offer alternative approaches to studying and learning from counterinsurgency, approaches that do account for the rules of social science. The vast majority of political scientists tend not to focus on insurgency as an area for social science inquiry. Political scientists are more apt to examine the causes of war or violence in general. However, these broad examinations often touch on insurgency as an aspect of war or violence. These broader studies often contain empirical findings relevant to the study of insurgency. This section will very briefly illustrate how political scientists use their unique methodologies to study insurgency and the causes of violence.

Two major works by political scientists that bear on the study of insurgency come at the problem from vastly different methodologies but arrive at surprisingly congruent conclusions. Jeffrey Herbst's examination of state formation and consolidation in Africa takes the classical political science approach of comparing and contrasting nation-states, in this case to understand why African states are so fragile or failing currently.[20] Herbst's extensive examination of African history and current affairs leads him to the conclusion that a logically justified lack of state penetration outside of major urban areas present in most African nations is leading to widespread violence, insurgency, and state failure.[21] Thus, while larger unifying themes, or religion and ethnicity, might seem to be driving violence in African states, a real impetus toward such violence are local grievances resulting from a lack of governmental service penetration. Each province, clan, or even village could be dealt with in a different manner depending on the service shortfall in their area.

Stathis Kalyvas conducted a groundbreaking microanalysis of a region of Greece during the Greek Civil War. He reconstructed violent action at the village level and empirically mapped this violence in order to better understand the motivations for violence in civil war.[22] Kalyvas found that macro-explanations for violence assumed a monolithic nature and motivation and attempted to group sides in a conflict broadly. Reality on the ground showed that civil war "often transforms local and personal grievances into lethal violence; once it occurs, this violence becomes endowed with a political meaning that may be quickly naturalized into new and enduring identities."[23] In other words, while it might seem after the conflict that the Serbs were fighting the Croats, at the micro-level, individuals may have been engaging in violence for profit or to settle a local grievance and the civil war or insurgency simply allowed them the opportunity to exploit this local tendency.

One prominent example of a political scientist examining insurgency specifically comes from Bard O'Neill. O'Neill captures almost the entire history of major insurgencies in the world and then constructs typologies out of this examination. O'Neill identifies nine types of insurgency and concludes that each type of insurgency requires a distinct counterinsurgency strategy.[24] Not only are these three studies rigorous in their analysis but they are steeped in the theoretical literature that preceded them. None of these political scientists posits they have the answer to collective violence. Instead, they couch their research in terms of their contribution to the literature or larger debate. It should also strike the reader that all three authors would be vehemently against the adoption of a single counterinsurgency approach and, unlike the population-centric proponents, they have the intensive research to back up their views.

Historians work with a slightly different methodology. Rather than explicitly hypothesize a universal truth and then research historical case studies to see how well the theory holds up, historians research an issue or a question and then write a narrative answer to that question. They do make generalizations, but, as John Gaddis has argued, they tend to embed those generalizations within the narratives.[25] The story and the argument go hand in hand. When it comes to military history, these sorts of generalizations are most common and evident in the study of conventional warfare. For example, generations of scholarship have produced a commonly agreed upon concept of Napoleonic warfare, emphasizing Bonaparte's use of staffs, mass armies organized into corps, aggressive offensives, dramatic maneuvers on campaign and in battle, and concentrated firepower in battle.[26] What historians have discovered, or at least what is evident from historical accounts of counterinsurgencies, is that the narratives and the generalizations differ enormously from case to case when it comes to counterinsurgency, so much so that most historians have avoided even trying to generalize about such wars.

The problem is evident in the work of the few historians who have attempted to draw larger conclusions from the study of small wars. For example, John Shy and Thomas W. Collier wrote a careful essay on "Revolutionary Warfare" in the 1986 version of *Makers of Modern Strategy* that tried to balance the historical record against dominant theoretical principles, in particular those found in the writings of Mao Zedong. Even as their account drew on examples from throughout the modern period, they treated revolutionary war as a discrete phenomenon of the twentieth century, one that was usually driven or inspired by communist ideology. Such a focus naturally excludes small wars inspired by other ideologies, but it is notable that even within Shy and Collier's relatively limited period of focus, they emphasized differences rather than similarities.[27] A more recent example is Mark Moyar, who used multiple historical case studies to make the case for counterinsurgency techniques built around leadership—finding and keeping military leaders who display initiative, flexibility, creativity, judgment, empathy, charisma, sociability, integrity, and organizational abilities. There is much to credit in Moyar's perspective, and it is well worth engaging. That said, it could be argued that his generalizations about leadership apply to any war, not just counterinsurgency. More importantly, he calls for leaders with the adaptability to apply unique techniques to specific circumstances, because few techniques appear to be universally applicable.[28]

A different but equally illustrative example is historian Andrew Birtle's two volumes covering U.S. Army counterinsurgency operations and doctrine from 1860 to 1976. Very few historical accounts have tried to survey counterinsurgencies over time in the manner of Birtle. In effect, his books propose something of an "American way of counterinsurgency," and his conclusions are telling. He is less explicit in his generalizations than either Shy and Collier or Moyar. He makes the case for the need to balance coercion and persuasion in any counterinsurgency, but, again, based on the specific circumstances of the given operation.[29]

The difficulty historians have had in deriving generalizations from the narratives of small wars is that broad theories of what works and does not work in such wars are too easily disproven by the specific examples; both within relatively narrow eras like the Cold War or even within discrete conflicts themselves. Under the ideological umbrella of the Cold War conflict, the context and conditions of the insurgencies in Malaya, Algeria, Vietnam, and so on vary wildly in key areas such as specific insurgent ideology (the degree of nationalism present), specific counterinsurgent objectives (colonial control, basic stability, democracy, etc.), fighting tactics of both sides (conventional, guerrilla, or both), the presence or absence of sanctuaries and the influx of outside resources, and the nature of the participation of greater powers on both sides. Even within specific wars, for example the Philippine Insurrection, successful counterinsurgent techniques differed in districts right next to each other on the island of Luzon and what worked one month within a district did not always work the next.[30]

Given all of these problems with both social scientific and historical methodologies, it is no wonder that military professionals have historically struggled with providing a clear vision for the training and education for small wars. Their time for training and education is limited by the everyday needs of running units, in peace almost as much as war. And even the portions of their careers dedicated specifically to study must account for more than just counterinsurgency.

So where does that leave us? Until social scientists can reliably isolate the factors that lead to success or historians can find more specific generalizations in their narratives, there are two related options. First, we can and must do our best to generalize about specific techniques for specific wars, and teach those generalizations and techniques to the military professionals set to engage in those wars. That method, despite any grandiose claims for its universality, was precisely the value of FM 3-24. That Counterinsurgency Manual was a necessary and important tool for fighting the war in Iraq at that time and within that context. However, as the subsequent experiences in Afghanistan have shown, FM 3-24's prescriptions are not transferable to all other situations. We need different techniques for that war, and it would be best to develop those solutions sooner rather than later.

This brings us to our second option. It is vital for all wars, but perhaps especially for counterinsurgencies, to foster a flexibility of mind among military professionals. That flexibility is best achieved through the study of multiple examples of counterinsurgency using varying analytical techniques, without prejudicing one presumed correct approach (whether it be population-centric or not) over others.[31] By learning how to think about the study of war, we will better know what to think, and do, about specific wars.[32] That has long been the premise of the education at the U.S. Army's School of Advanced Military Studies, and that, in short, is what this anthology of monographs from students at the school proposes to do.

The Case Studies

The case studies begin with an example using a political science methodology, written by Major Kenneth D. Mitchell. In "Failed State: A New (Old) Definition," Mitchell looked at the notion of failed states. He began by examining all of the major state ranking systems as well as the lexicon of definitions of failed states. All of these ranking systems were found to carry a heavy bias towards higher-end development, like the development of human rights, rather than focusing on foundational aspects of state development, like safety, security, and rule of law. This allowed for conundrums to occur, like the Mexican case, in which a state has clearly ceded sovereignty and lost basic control over several key provinces and yet continually garners a high ranking on the various failed state indices. This bias mirrors the current bias in population-centric counterinsurgency which emphasizes the need for nation-building even when fundamental security considerations are not in place.

Mitchell concluded from his empirical investigation of the failed state ranking systems and his analysis of Mexican state fragility that a state must structure the delivery of public goods in a sequential and hierarchical basis with safety, security, and rule of law providing a foundation upon which all other higher-end public goods rest. He further posited that the needs for foundational security are so great that military coercion or a kinetic clamp-down may be necessary in order to lay a timely foundation upon which other activities rest. The premature focus on participation and human rights can create weak and illegitimate state institutions since safety and security do not form the foundation of the state's contract.

"Toward Development of Afghanistan National Stability: Analyses in Historical, Military, and Cultural Contexts," by Lieutenant Colonel Christopher D. Dessaso takes a slightly different approach. Dessaso takes another look at the history of governance in Afghanistan, but rather than focus on attempts by outside powers to assert control within that war torn land, he evaluates the effectiveness of various centralized Afghan governing regimes. His examples range from the mid-nineteenth century through the twentieth century, and in each case he looks at the way governance, military power, economics, and social issues interacted to determine the degree to which the various centralized governments exerted control over the country as a whole. Contrary to the conventional wisdom that Afghanistan has always been entirely fractured, several of these regimes did quite well in consolidating power and even attempting modernizing reforms. However, he did identify a unifying theme that dovetails with Mitchell's findings: the most successful regimes maintained strong control of the national military and consolidation of the central government. Those governments that attempted to modernize or reform without control of the military inevitably failed, even if the general population looked favorably upon the attempted reforms.

The final case study, written by Major Jose R. Laguna, is a more direct questioning of the major theory behind the population centric approach. In "Algerian Perspectives of Counterinsurgencies," Laguna returns to Algeria, the country that provided the experiences behind David Galula's theories of counterinsurgency. But while Galula focused solely on France's (his own) war from 1954 to 1962, Laguna widens his lens to look at a broader view of Algerian history. He begins with the French war, in order to better understand that conflict and how it spawned the theories of Galula and others prominent theorists, especially Roger Trinquier. In so doing, he illustrates one of the conundrums of modern counterinsurgency theory. Namely, if Galula and his compatriots managed to identify principles of a successful counterinsurgency in Algeria, why is it that France ultimately lost their war for the country? His answer lies in large part in the oft-maligned and misunderstood concept of levels of war. The bulk of Galula's theory focuses on mostly tactical and occasionally operational considerations, the French failed strategically in the war by opting for a direct intervention that became increasingly unpopular at home.

Laguna contrasts that experience with Ottoman rule in North Africa, and finds that one of the main reasons the Ottomans managed to maintain control for so long was because they made the strategic choice not to intervene directly and get involved in a tactical counterinsurgency. Rather, they determined that their larger interests did not require direct intervention, so they controlled elites and played competing factions off of one another. A similar dynamic was at play in the Algerian Civil War from 1991-2002, Laguna's next area of focus. After years of strife and difficulty, the government finally quelled the threat of Islamic extremists. They did so again not by directly getting involved in winning over the population, but by focusing on eliminating extremist leadership, controlling information, and playing on divisions between various factions throughout the country. As it turned out, in Algeria, the very font of population-centric counterinsurgency theory and doctrine, the best alternative in defeating insurgency was not to get involved with the population at all.

Some Tentative Conclusions

As will be obvious from a close reading, the theory and the practice of population-centric focus is not really sustained in these case studies. And the problems with an overreliance on the population-centric approach do not stop here. Part of the theoretical foundation of the population-centric approach comes from the British, and in turn their theories were based on the successful campaign in Malaya (1948-1960). The Counterinsurgency Manual explicitly cites Robert Thompson and Frank Kitson, and it also shows the influence of the thinking of Julian Paget, all of whom discussed the importance of winning 'hearts and minds', at least with the implication that this meant a less violent or coercive approach. Nagl, one of the driving forces behind FM 3-24, made a similar case in his book on counterinsurgency.[33] But even if we accept that the unique conditions of Malaya translate to other times and places, the reality is that if the British effort won hearts and minds, it did so every bit as much through coercion and repression as it did through more subtle means of convincing the population.[34]

Put simply, one would be hard-pressed to find an example of a counterinsurgency that worked on an entirely or even majority persuasive model. An insurgency by definition means that violence has already broken out, and once that step has been taken, it is almost impossible to take back. That is why the organized use of violence toward a purpose, and the organized active use of violence to resist that purpose, represent a separate category of human affairs we call war. It is a separate category because the presence of actual violence, as opposed to just the threat, releases emotions that change the rules of human interaction.[35] Under those rules, once those emotions have been loosed, it is nearly impossible to persuade an enemy to lay down arms. Coercion, *applied violence*, must play a role, however contrary it runs to the perceived initial causes of the war, and however distasteful it might seem. Unfortunately, that role appears to be greater than what the population centric theory and doctrine lets on.

But again, how great depends on the specific circumstances and again, there are no simple answers here, and in no way do the three case studies that follow represent all that is to be said on the issues of small wars. Their varying approaches to multiple examples are simply a good start to a type of learning about small wars for military professionals—a learning that cannot and must never stop.

Notes

1. US Army Field Manual 3-24, *Counterinsurgency* (Washington, DC: Department of the Army, 2006).

2. Andrew F. Krepinevich, Jr., *The Army and Vietnam* (Baltimore, MD: Johns Hopkins University Press, 1986).

3. David H. Ucko, *The New Counterinsurgency Era: Transforming the U. S. Military for Modern Wars* (Washington, DC: Georgetown University Press, 2009). See also Max Boot, *The Savage Wars of Peace: Small Wars and the Rise of American Power* (New York: Basic Books, 2002), and Robert M. Cassidy, "Back to the Street without Joy: Counterinsurgency Lessons from Vietnam and Other Small Wars," *Parameters*, 34 (Summer 2004), 73-83, among others.

4. Lewis Sorley, *A Better War: The Unexamined Victories and Final Tragedy of America's Last Years in Vietnam* (New York: Harcourt Brace, 1999); and Sorley, "To Change a War: General Harold K. Johnson and the PROVN Study," *Parameters*, 28 (Spring 1998), 93-109.

5. Harry G. Summers, *On Strategy* (New York: Dell, 1984).

6. Dale Andrade, "Westmoreland was right: learning the wrong lessons from the Vietnam War," *Small Wars and Insurgencies*, 19 (June 2008), 145-181; and Andrew J. Birtle, "PROVN, Westmoreland, and the Historians: A Reappraisal," *Journal of Military History*, 72 (October 2008), 1213-1247.

7. David Galula, *Counterinsurgency Warfare: Theory and Practice* (New York: Praeger Publishers, 1968), 95.

8. John A. Nagl, "Constructing the Legacy of Field Manual 3-24," *Joint Force Quarterly*, (3d Quarter, 2010), 118. See also, John A. Nagl, *Learning to Eat Soup with a Knife: Counterinsurgency Lessons from Malaya and Vietnam* (Chicago, IL: University of Chicago Press, 2005).

9. Robert M. Cassidy, "Indigenous Forces and Sanctuary Denial: Enduring Counterinsurgency Imperatives," *Small Wars Journal*, http://smallwarsjournal.com/mag/docs-temp/44-cassidy.pdf.

10. Robert M. Cassidy, "Winning the War of the Flea: Lessons from Guerilla Warfare," *Military Review*, 84 (September-October 2004), 41-46.

11. Heather S. Gregg, "Beyond Population Engagement: Understanding Counterinsurgency," *Parameters*, 39 (Autumn 2009), 18.

12. Gian P. Gentile, "A Strategy of Tactics: Population-Centric COIN and the Army," *Parameters*, 39 (Autumn 2009), 6; and. Gentile, "Let's Build an Army to Win *All* Wars," *Joint Force Quarterly*, (1st Quarter, 2009), 27.

13. Gentile, "Strategy of Tactics," 8.

14. Ibid.

15. Galula, *Counterinsurgency Warfare*, 65; Frank Kitson, *Low Intensity Operations: Subversion, Insurgency, and Peacekeeping* (St. Petersburg, FL: Hailer Publishing, 1971), 67; and Bard E. O'Neill, *Insurgency and Terrorism: From Revolution to Apocalypse*, 2nd edition revised (Washington, DC: Potomac Books, 2005), 155-58.

16. Galula, *Counterinsurgency Warfare*, 54.

17. Carl von Clausewitz, *On War*, edited and translated by Michael Howard and Peter Paret (Princeton, NJ: Princeton University Press, 1976), Sun Tsu, *The Art of War*, translated by Samuel B. Griffith with a foreword by B. H. Liddell Hart, (Oxford University Press, 1971), and Galula, *Counterinsurgency Warfare*, to name but a few.

18. Paul David Reynolds, *A Primer in Theory Construction* (New Jersey: Prentice Hall, 1971).

19. Gian P. Gentile, "A Strategy of Tactics," 6.

20. Jeffrey Herbst, *States and Power in Africa: Comparative Lessons in Authority and Control* (Princeton, NJ: Princeton University Press, 2000), 13.

21. Jeffrey Herbst, 254.

22. Stathis N. Kalyvas, *The Logic of Violence in Civil War* (New York: Cambridge University Press, 2006), 247.

23. Stathis N. Kalyvas, 389.

24. Bard E. O'Neill, *Insurgency and Terrorism: From Revolution to Apocalypse*, 2nd revised edition (Washington, DC: Potomac Books, 2005), 20-29.

25. John Lewis Gaddis, *The Landscape of History: How Historians Map the Past* (New York: Oxford University Press, 2002).

26. See, for example, David G. Chandler, *The Campaigns of Napoleon* (New York: Macmillan, 1966); Gunther E. Rothenberg, *The Art of Warfare in the Age of Napoleon* (Bloomington: Indiana University Press, 1978); Russell F. Weigley, *The Age of Battles: The Quest for Decisive Warfare from Breitenfeld to Waterloo* (Bloomington: Indiana University Press, 1991); Owen Connelly, *Blundering to Glory: Napoleon's Military Campaigns* (Wilmington, DE: Scholarly Resources, 1987); and Robert M. Epstein, *Napoleon's Last Victory and the Emergence of Modern War* (Lawrence: University Press of Kansas, 1994).

27. John Shy and Thomas W. Collier, "Revolutionary War," in *Makers of Modern Strategy: From Machiavelli to the Nuclear Age*, edited by Peter Paret (Princeton, NJ: Princeton University Press, 1986), 815-862.

28. Mark Moyar, *A Question of Command: Counterinsurgency from the Civil War to Iraq* (New Haven, CT: Yale University Press, 2009).

29. Andrew J. Birtle, *US Army Counterinsurgency and Contingency Operations Doctrine, 1860-1941* (Washington DC: US Army Center of Military History, 2004), *US Army Counterinsurgency and Contingency Operations Doctrine, 1942-1976* (Washington DC: US Army Center of Military History, 2006), and "Persuasion and Coercion in Counterinsurgency Warfare," *Military Review*, 88 (July-August 2008), 45-53.

30. See especially, Brian McAllister Linn, *The US Army and Counterinsurgency in the Philippine War, 1899-1902* (Chapel Hill: University of North Carolina Press, 1989), and Robert D. Ramsey, *Savage Wars of Peace: Case Studies of Pacification in the Philippines, 1900-1902*, Long War Series Occasional Paper 24 (Fort Leavenworth, KS: Combat Studies Institute Press, 2007).

31. A good example is Brian McAllister Linn, "The US Army and Nation Building and Pacification in the Philippines," in *Armed Diplomacy: Two Centuries of American Campaigning* (Fort Leavenworth, KS: Combat Studies Institute Press, 2003), 77-89.

32. Examples of the argument of teaching how to think include Richard E. Neustadt and Ernest R. May, *Thinking in Time: The Uses of History for Decision Makers* (New York: Free Press, 1986); Jay Luvaas, "Military History: Is It Still Practicable?" *Parameters*, 12 (March 1982), 2-14; Antulio J. Echevarria, "The Trouble with History," *Parameters*, 35 (Summer 2005), 78-90; and Jacob Shuford, "Re-Education for the 21st-Century Warrior," *United States Naval Institute Proceedings*, 135 (April 2009), 14-19.

33. Nagl, *Learning to Eat Soup*.

34. See, for example, Paul Dixon, "'Hearts and Minds'? British Counter-Insurgency from Malaya to Iraq," *Journal of Strategic Studies*, 32 (June 2009), 353-381.

35. Clausewitz, *On War*, passim; and to a lesser extent John Keegan, *A History of Warfare* (New York: Alfred A Knopf, 1993).

Failed State: A New (Old) Definition

Major Kenneth D. Mitchell

This monograph posits that the state must structure the delivery of public goods in a sequential and hierarchical basis with safety and security and rule of law providing a foundation upon which the state builds delivery of all other public goods prior to any discussion of higher level needs like participation and human rights. In support of this premise, this monograph defines a failed state as a state which *cannot* claim a monopoly on the legitimate use of physical force within a given territory.

This research explores various state ranking systems, which purport to measure state delivery of public goods. These measurements are aggregated and interpreted to assess state fragility. These ranking systems carry a bias toward higher end development, like the development of human rights, rather than focusing on foundational aspects of state development, like safety, security, and rule of law. Mexico illustrates this monograph's thesis by showing that performance in other categories of governance cannot offset a lack safety and security for the citizens of Mexico. The implication of this premature focus on participation and human rights is the creation of weak and illegitimate state institutions since safety and security did not form the foundation of the state's contract.

Introduction

Talk of failed or failing states dominates current US foreign policy. The United States justified its military intervention in Somalia, Bosnia, Haiti (1994), Afghanistan, and Iraq with the concept of failed or failing states. The United States further justified these military interventions with the premise that failing states pose a risk to US national interests through ungoverned space in which non-state extremist actors can plan, operate, and launch attacks on the United States. When a state cannot provide safety and security to its citizenry or control its own territory by exercising the rule of law through police, prisons, and a judiciary, that state has the risk for giving rise to safe haven for non-state actors and the associated terrorism. However, it is difficult to define the criteria for which a state is classified as 'failed.' A state exists to provide public goods to its citizens. Thus, a failed state is unable or unwilling to provide those public goods to its citizens. This paper groups the public goods provided by a state into five categories: participation and human rights, human development, economic development, rule of law, and safety and security.

However, major differences exist between research institutions on the content and scope of the public goods a state should provide. Based on US efforts in Iraq and Afghanistan, the main effort of US foreign policy after military interventions in failed states is the delivery of participation and human rights. This foreign policy focus is based on mistaken assumptions. The state must structure the delivery of public goods in a sequential and hierarchical basis with safety and security and rule of law providing a foundation upon which the state builds delivery of all other public goods prior to any discussion of higher level needs like participation and human rights. For example, a citizen cannot start a business to improve his economic position in a war-time environment or one in which murder is rampant. Education and human development cannot exist in an environment in which criminals kill or maim citizens attempting to go to school. Participation in the political process cannot occur in an environment where the act of voting puts one at risk for death or bodily harm. The state must achieve safety and security prior to pursuing any of the other state roles.

This research explores the impact of these indices, which purport to measure state delivery of public goods. These measurements are aggregated and interpreted to assess state fragility. The problem with this analysis is that these scores come mainly from modern western conceptions of the state's role, which carry a bias toward higher end development, like the development of human rights, rather than focusing on foundational aspects of state development, like safety, security, and rule of law. For this reason, it is important to explore these indices in detail because policymakers often make decisions to intervene based on reports of state fragility. It is of paramount importance to ensure that the right intellectual construct is used to measure state fragility. Mexico illustrates this monograph's thesis by showing that good performance in other categories of governance cannot offset a lack of safety and security for the citizens of Mexico. The implication of US foreign policy's premature focus on participation and human rights is the creation of weak and illegitimate state institutions that will fail once US forces depart since safety and security did not form the foundation of the state's contract.

One of the author's main focuses will be a discussion of the definition of a state and thus the definition of a failed state. To provide background, this paper will examine the philosophical and historical growth of the state. Following this discussion, the author will review the various state ranking systems used to categorize a stable or failing state. These ranking systems consistently assess state performance through the delivery of public goods to its citizens. Finally, the author examines Mexico, to determine whether Mexico represents a failed state. A single country study is comparative since US foreign policy can apply concepts illustrated with respect to Mexico to other potential failed and failing states. The inferences regarding failed states stretch beyond Mexico to the entire international community.[1]

The Philosophical Progression of the Nature of a Sovereign State

The term failed state is very ambiguous. Noam Chomsky controversially defines failed state in such a manner that the United States is a failed state. His contested definition is a state which is unable to protect its citizens from violence and a state not concerned with international laws and norms.[2] He claims the United States, through its actions during the War on Terror, has actually made its citizens more vulnerable to terrorist attack – thus failing to protect its citizens from violence. In addition, Chomsky claims US actions in Iraq and Afghanistan violate international norms. Many debate his analysis but it illustrates an important point; by vaguely defining the term failed state, one can argue for military intervention in any number of third (or first) world countries. Decision makers require a strict and narrow definition of the term 'failed state' to make sound policy judgments. However, in order to define a failed state, one must first define a state and this is a step often overlooked by scholars.

Philosophical Basis of the State

The concept of the state arose in Europe during the late Middle Ages. Philosophers and political scientists refined the concept of the state over time; culminating in the American Revolution. Much of the development of the concept of the state as an abstract entity resulted from the enlightenment and new ways of thinking about rulers and their relationship to the ruled. In all cases, the philosopher tried to answer the question, "What is the best way to create order in human society?" The main philosophers responsible for the philosophical underpinnings of the state are Erasmus, Machiavelli, Jean Bodin, Cardin la Bret, Hobbes, Locke, and Montesquieu. Figure 1 shows the philosophers' time periods, major writings, and major wars relevant to the modern concept of the state.

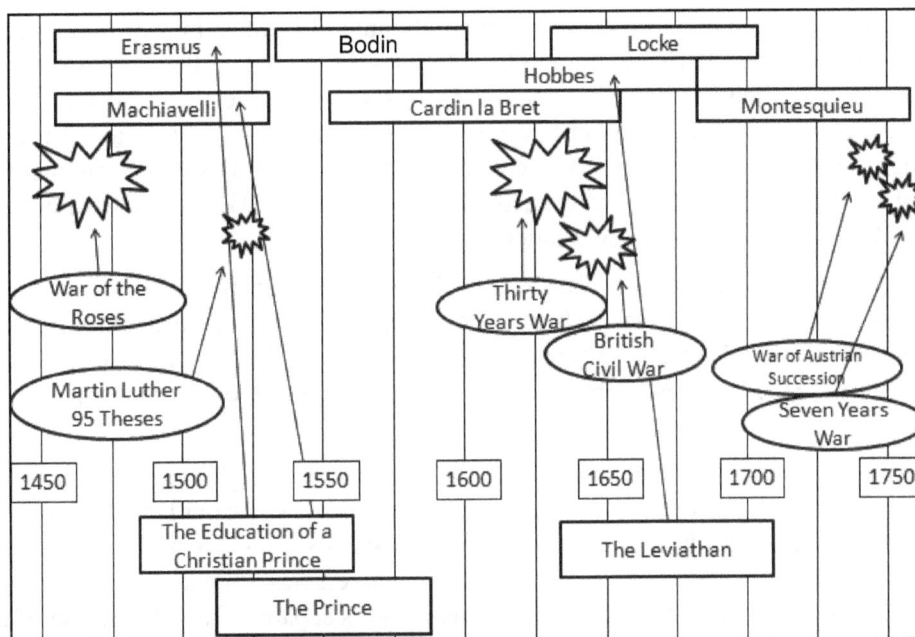

Figure 1: Philosophical evolution of the state.[3]

In the early Middle Ages, the relationship between the sovereign and the people under his rule was that of a god to a slave. The sovereign could not be corrupt or unjust since the sovereign was the ruler by divine right. The sovereign, the person, was the government. There was no separation between his personal identity and his role as head of the government. In 1516, Erasmus, a Dutch philosopher, published *The Education of a Christian Prince*. In this work, Erasmus set forth the premise that a ruler should be concerned with good and justice.[4] The people's love would be the measure of the sovereign's performance. However, he still viewed the sovereign's right to rule as divine. Thus an unjust ruler still maintains his divine position as sovereign unanswerable to the people.

Machiavelli was an Italian philosopher whose most notable work was *The Prince*. He maintained the ruler's divine right to rule but contrasted with Erasmus's view of a ruler's purpose. He argued that a 'good' ruler did not need piety and justice but instead required force and guile.[5] A good sovereign was better feared than loved. Force and guile would allow the ruler to obtain what was in the best interest of the nation regardless of the morals of the individual situation; politics by any means necessary. Machiavelli separated the role and responsibilities of the sovereign from judgments concerning good and bad or right and wrong.

Following Erasmus and Machiavelli, Jean Bodin added to the modern concept of the state. His additions were prompted by the historical context of the time. In 1517, Martin Luther posted his 95 Theses.[6] This action ignited the Protestant Reformation. With the nature and identity of God in dispute throughout Europe, Bodin rejected the divine nature of Erasmus's sovereign and also rejected the coldly amoral justifications of Machiavelli. Bodin posited that the ruler's most important duty lay in upholding the rule of law.[7] In addition, he argued convincingly that one could not serve two sovereigns. This broke the old feudal ties which created conflict throughout European history. At the same time, by divorcing the sovereign from God, Bodin collapsed all political entities superior to the state (those of church and empire). Shortly thereafter, the Treaty of Westphalia solidified the primacy of the state in international relations.

A French jurist, Cardin la Bret, was the first philosopher to separate the ruler's personal identity from his role as sovereign and head of government. He defined a difference between treason against the king's person and treason versus the state.[8] Prior to this distinction, the ruler was the state incarnate. Now the ruler was just the figurehead for a new abstract entity, the state.

Building on the concept of the state as an abstract entity, Hobbes published *The Leviathan*. Hobbes defined man as existing in a state of nature where our lives are "solitary, poore, nasty, brutish, and short."[9] Man fears and thus spends his whole life seeking power over his fellow man. To escape this state of nature, man creates a social contract with the state. Hobbes defines the state as an artificial man who is separate from the person of the ruler or sovereign. The sovereign carries the state and rules in its name. Without the state's enforcement of the social contract, man will slip back into the state of nature where there is no law. Law can only exist within the structure provided by the state. For Hobbes, like Machiavelli, the state is amoral and governs in the best way to maintain public order. The state, with military, police, and prisons, becomes the Leviathan. Any abuses by the government are simply the price paid to escape the state of nature.

Locke came to the same conclusions as Hobbes regarding the formulation of the state as an abstract, powerful entity separate from that of the sovereign. However, Locke approaches the problem with a different assumption concerning man's nature. Hobbes assumes than man's nature is to follow his desires and passions. The state must restrain man from the state of nature and war of all against all.[10] Locke posits that man's reason leads him to what he calls enlightened self-interest.[11] This enlightened self-interest allows man to live in peace most of the time. Thus it is the government's job not to constrain man, but to safeguard the rights man had been endowed; "no one ought to harm another in his life, health, liberty, or possessions."[12] Civil society created the state out of enlightened self-interest to defend its rights from internal and external threats.

The final philosopher leading the modern definition and formulation of the state is Montesquieu. Montesquieu based his ideas upon Hume's conception of the nature of human reason. Hume posited that "Reason is, and ought only to be the slave of the passions, and can never pretend to any other office than to serve and obey them."[13] For Locke, reason was absolute. Hume believed that reason was subjective. Accepting reason as subjective, Montesquieu postulated that laws must be the basis of government; subjective laws made by man so that "one man need not be afraid of another."[14] He completed the process by which the force of laws other than those of the state was abolished. From this point, laws (good or bad) were simply those which the state enacted. Laws and the state were both amoral. With Montesquieu, the theoretical structure of the state was complete.

Erasmus started with a divine sovereign that ruled with justice. Machiavelli gave us a divine sovereign that was amoral. Bodin gave us the rule of law. La Bret created the state as an abstract entity separate from the sovereign. Hobbes and Locke both gave us an all-powerful state to protect us from external and internal threats (one to constrain man and the other to safeguard man's rights). Finally, Montesquieu gave us rule of law whose origin was of man not divine.

In summary, the state is an all-powerful entity tearing down all laws except those created by the state itself. God and nature are divorced from the state. The state does not have to observe custom and is capable of doing anything. From this construct, the state was the most powerful political construct ever created. It owns the military, police, and prison system and uses them as tools to create order and protect its citizens from internal and external threats; to impose order amongst the interaction of the citizens. Thus the role of the state from a philosophical perspective was as Max Weber stated, "the state is a human community that (successfully) claims the monopoly of the legitimate use of physical force within a given territory."[15] According to the above philosophical basis, a failed state is a state which *cannot* claim a monopoly on the legitimate use of physical force within a given territory. Therefore, safety and security is the original and most important public good delivered by a state to its citizens.

Measuring the State and thus Failed States

Since the inception of the United Nations (UN) and even prior with the League of Nations, there has been a desire by the developed countries of the world to help and assist developing nation's progress and become more like the developed world. Nothing in the realm of international politics is done out of benevolence if viewed through the lens of realism.[16] The reason that the developed world helps the developing world is because they feel it is in their national interest. This national interest is related to the concept of the democratic peace as espoused in our current National Security Strategy, "Because democracies are the most responsible members of the international system, promoting democracy is the most effective long-term measure for strengthening international stability;

reducing regional conflicts; countering terrorism and terror-supporting extremism; and extending peace and prosperity."[17] Through this lens, the United States views democracies as inherently more stable than autocratic or semi-authoritarian regimes.[18] This view is not universally held and opposes the construct in which safety and security are the primary role of the state. The columnist and bestselling author, Fareed Zakaria, claims that democracies are "more warlike, going to war more often and with greater intensity than most states. It is only with other democracies that the peace holds."[19]

To assist the developing world in a progression to a more democratic ideal, various organizations have created indices to rank governance. The stated purpose of these indices and ranking systems varies. Some state that the purpose for ranking is to set standards for improvement and achievement, as well as indicate where funds could be of best use, and which policies might prove most effective. Others suggest that the indices can act as a shaming mechanism or as political leverage by elites to mobilize their constituents, thus encouraging open debate.[20] Finally, organizations justify monetary aid based on these rankings; organizations such as United States Agency for International Development (USAID), the International Monetary Fund (IMF), the Millennium Challenge Account, the World Bank, the United Nations (UN), and the European Union (EU) all base aid on performance measures associated with the various ranking systems.

Each ranking system views governance as the delivery of public goods but differs in the framework and content. This paper will categorize the various public goods discussed by the indices into five categories: (1) Participation and Human Rights, (2) Human Development, (3) Economic Development, (4) Rule of Law, and (5) Safety and Security. This paper will review the following indices: Freedom House's Freedom in the World Index (FIW), the Center for Systemic Peace's Polity IV Index, the World Bank's Worldwide Governance Research Indicators Dataset (WGI), the World Economic Forum's Global Governance Initiative (GGI), the Overseas Development Institute's World Governance Assessment (WGA), the UN's African Governance Report (AGR), the Kennedy School of Government's Index of African Governance (IAG), and the Fund for Peace's Failed State Index (FSI).[21] The following section will give a short history and background for each ranking system.

Most of the ranking systems base their evaluation of state performance on subjective measures utilizing household and firm surveys, commercial business information providers, non-governmental organizations, and public sector organizations. The ranking systems which utilize subjective measures justify this approach with three supporting premises. First, perceptions matter because people base their actions on their perceptions. Second, there are few alternatives to perception data for many areas of governance. Third, the distinction between subjective and objective data may be a false one. A more useful distinction would be between efforts to measure formal rules as opposed to those rules implemented in practice. Other ranking systems attempt to utilize more concrete, measurable data. For example, the Index of African Governance is an example of an index which attempts to avoid all subjective data, utilizing only quantifiable measures of performance when possible.

16

The Freedom in the World (FIW) ranking system created by the Freedom House started in 1972 and ranks countries as Free, Partly Free, and Not Free. It utilizes subjective measures to look at political rights and civil rights.[22] The organization claims that it does not maintain a culture bound interpretation of freedom. However, it does base its definition of freedom on the UN Declaration of Human Rights.[23] This represents a western view of human rights based on the Judeo-Christian tradition. Islamic countries have boycotted the UN Declaration of Human Rights in favor of the Cairo Declaration of Human Rights.[24] Thus, the FIW ranking may have limited utility throughout the Islamic world. This index heavily weights the category of participation and human rights.

Table 1: Freedom in the World.

Category of Public Goods	Freedom in the World		
Participation and Human Rights	Political Rights		
		Electoral Process	
		Political Pluralism and Participation	
		Functioning of Government	
	Civil Liberties		
		Freedom of Expression and Belief	
		Associational and Organizational Rights	
		Personal Autonomy and Individual Rights	
Human Development	Not addressed		
Economic Development			
Rule of Law	Rule of Law		
Safety and Security	Not addressed		

Source: Author's interpretation and categorization of the Freedom in the World methodology.[25]

The Center for Systemic Peace started the Polity index in the late 1960s[26] and refined it up to the current version of Polity IV in 2008.[27] This index views the global system as a black box.[28] States operate within the black box but are complex systems of their own which are "self-actuating, self-organizing, self-regulating, and self-correcting."[29] State performance is assessed among three interconnected dimensions of governance, conflict, and development.

Governance is composed of political effectiveness and political legitimacy. Similarly, conflict is composed of security effectiveness and legitimacy. Development incorporates two subcategories, economic and social. Each subcategory is assessed according to its effectiveness and legitimacy. The fragility index is a combination of the above measures. This index presents a broad assessment of the categories of public goods but neglects the category rule of law.

Table 2: Polity IV Index.

Category of Public Goods	Polity IV	
Participation and Human Rights	Political Legitimacy	
		Regime Inclusion
		Factionalism
		Ethnic Group Political Discrimination
		Political Salience of Elite Ethnicity
		Polity Fragmentation
		Exclusionary Ideology of Ruling Elite
	Security Legitimacy – state repression	
Human Development	Social Effectiveness – human capital development	
	Social Legitimacy – infant mortality rate	
Economic Development	Economic Effectiveness – GDP per capita	
	Economic Legitimacy - % export trade in man. goods	
Rule of Law	Not addressed	
Safety and Security	Security Effectiveness – total residual war	
	Political Effectiveness – regime stability	

Source: Author's interpretation and categorization of the Polity methodology.[30]

The World Bank's Worldwide Governance Research Indicators Dataset (WGI) started in 1996 and defines good governance as a "set of traditions and institutions by which authority in a country is exercised for the common good."[31]

Table 3: Worldwide Governance Indicator.

Category of Public Goods	Worldwide Governance Indicator
Participation and Human Rights	Voice and Accountability
Human Development	Not addressed
Economic Development	
Rule of Law	Rule of Law
	Control of Corruption
	Regulatory Quality
	Government Effectiveness
Safety and Security	Political Stability

Source: Author's interpretation and categorization of the Worldwide Governance Indicators methodology.[32]

This includes (1) the process by which those in authority are selected, monitored and replaced, (2) the capacity of the government to effectively manage its resources and implement sound policies, and (3) the respect of citizens and the state for the institutions that govern economic and social interactions among them.[33] This index is heavily weighted towards rule of law and evaluates voice and accountability, rule of law, control of corruption, regulatory quality, government effectiveness, and political stability.

The World Economic Forum created the Global Governance Initiative (GGI) in 2006[34] to monitor the efforts of governments, the private sector, international organizations, and civil society towards achieving the United Nations Millennium Development Goals.[35]

Table 4: Global Governance Initiative.

Category of Public Goods	Global Governance Initiative	UN Millennium Challenge	
Participation and Human Rights	Human Rights	Gender Equality	Source: Author's interpretation and categorization of the Global Governance Initiative methodology.[36]
Human Development	Poverty and Hunger	End Poverty and Hunger	
	Health	Child Health	
		Maternal Health	
		Combat HIV/AIDS	
	Education	Universal Education	
Economic Development	Environment	Environmental Sustainability	
		Global Partnership	
Rule of Law	Not addressed		
Safety and Security	Peace and Security	Not addressed	

Table 5: World Governance Assessment.

Category of Public Goods	World Governance Assessment	
Participation and Human Rights	Political Society	Source: Author's interpretation and categorization of the World Governance Assessment methodology.[37]
	Civil Society	
Human Development	Not addressed	
Economic Development	Economic Society	
Rule of Law	Judiciary	
	Bureaucracy	
	Government	
Safety and Security	Not addressed	

The eight goals of the Millennium Challenge are to eradicate extreme hunger and poverty, achieve universal primary education, promote gender equality and empower women, reduce child mortality, improve maternal health, combat HIV, malaria, and other diseases, ensure environmental sustainability, and develop a global partnership for development. The GGI neglects the global partnerships aspect of the Millennium Challenge and adds a category of peace and security. It broadens gender equality to human rights, and groups the three health related goals into one overall health category. This index is heavily weighted towards the category of human development.

The Overseas Development Institute is Britain's leading independent think tank on international development and humanitarian issues.[38] It has developed the World Governance Assessment (WGA) which defines governances as "how the rules of the political games are managed."[39] This index examines political society, civil society, economic society, the judiciary, bureaucracy, and government.

The UN's Economic Commission for Africa commissioned the African Governance Report (AGR) and defines the core elements of good governance as "political governance, institutional effectiveness, and accountability, and economic management and corporate governance."[40] It defines a capable state as one with transparent and accountable political and economic systems with efficient public institutions providing an enabling environment for the private sector and civil society to play their respective roles in national efforts.

Table 6: African Governance Report.

Category of Public Goods	African Governance Report
Participation and Human Rights	Political Governance
	Human Rights and Rule of Law
Human Development	Not addressed
Economic Development	Economic Governance and Public Financial Management
	Private Sector Development and Corporate Governance
Rule of Law	Institutional Checks and Balances
	Institutional Effectiveness and Accountability of the Executive
Safety and Security	Not addressed
Misc.	Institutional Capacity Building for Good Governance

Source: Author's interpretation and categorization of the African Governance Report methodology.[41]

This index examines political governance, human rights and rule of law,[42] economic governance and public financial management, private sector development and corporate governance, institutional checks and balances, institutional effectiveness and accountability of the executive and institutional capacity building for good governance.[43]

Table 7: Index of African Governance.

Category of Public Goods	Index of African Governance	
Participation and Human Rights	Participation and Human Rights	
		Participation in Elections
		Respect for Civil and Political Rights
Human Development	Human Development	
		Poverty
		Health and Sanitation
		Education
Economic Development	Sustainable Economic Opportunity	
		Wealth Creation
		Macroeconomic Stability and Financial Integrity
		The Arteries of Commerce
		Environmental Sensitivity
Rule of Law	Rule of Law, Transparency, and Corruption	
		Ratification of Critical Legal Norms
		Judicial Independence and Efficiency
		Corruption
Safety and Security	Safety and Security	
		National Security
		Public Safety

Source: Author's interpretation and categorization of the Index of African Governance methodology.[44]

The Kennedy School of Government and the World Peace Foundation[45] created the Index of African Governance (IAG).[46] The project split into two separate rankings systems, the original Index of African Governance and the newer Ibrahim Index.[47] Currently both indexes are published with slight differences. Due to the similarities and intellectual heritage, this paper will only address the IAG. This index builds its evaluation on the premise that states "exist to provide a decentralized method of delivering political (public) goods to persons living within designated parameters.... It is according to their performances – according to the levels of their effective delivery of the most crucial political goods – that strong states may be distinguished from weak ones."[48] The Index of African Governance is a robust index assessing all five categories of public goods.

The final index is the Failed States Index (FSI) created by the Fund for Peace.[49] It ranks countries on a continuum of state failures. The Failed State Index bases its assessment on the conflict assessment system tool (CAST) created and patented by Pauline H. Baker in 1996.[50] The CAST model utilizes four sources to assess the potential for conflict in a region; (1) ranking twelve social, economic, political, and military indicators, (2) assessing the capabilities of five core state institutions, (3) identifying idiosyncratic factors and surprises, and (4) placing countries on a conflict map that shows the risk history of countries being analyzed.[51]

Table 8: Failed State Index.

Category of Public Goods	Failed State Index
Participation and Human Rights	Group Grievance
	Factionalized Elites
	Legitimacy of the State
	Human Rights
Human Development	Mounting Demographic Pressures
	Public Services
Economic Development	Uneven Development
	Economic Decline
Rule of Law	Not addressed
Safety and Security	Security Apparatus
	External Intervention
	Refugees and IDP
	Human Flight

Source: Author's interpretation and categorization of the Failed State Index methodology.[52]

Analyzing the Indices by Areas of Governance

This section will review the eight ranking systems according to their treatment of the categories of participation and human rights, human development, economic development, rule of law, and safety and security. Table 9 shows an overview of each index's coverage of the various categories of public goods. The category of participation and human rights is the most commonly assessed category with all eight indices evaluating state performance in the delivery of that public good. This commonality contrasts starkly with the treatment for the category of safety and security with only two of eight indices assessing that category in a robust manner.

Participation and Human Rights

Participation encapsulates the public good of political freedom. It includes the ability to participate freely in politics, regardless of ethnicity, gender, social status, or other group markers. When government is working well, political participation means that the provision of public goods reflect the preferences of the citizens. Political participation can take a variety of forms, from individual communications with elected officials to mass protests, from consensus decision making in village or town meetings to active deliberation between citizen groups and members of government.[53] The human rights aspect of this category focuses on civil and political rights. Karel Vasak calls these "first generation rights"[54] such as freedom of speech and religion. Every index ranks states according to performance in regard to participation and human rights.

Table 9: Overall index coverage of the categories of public goods.

	Participation and Human Rights	Human Development	Economic Development	Rule of Law	Safety and Security	
FIW	Y	N	N	Y	N	
Polity	Y	Y	Y	N	Marginal	
WGI	Marginal	N	N	Y	Marginal	
GGI	Marginal	Y	Marginal	N	Marginal	
WGA	Y	N	Y	Y	N	
AGR	Y	N	Y	Y	N	
IAG	Y	Y	Y	Y	Y	
FSI	Y	Y	Y	N	Y	

Freedom in the World (FIW) evaluates participation through the sub-categories electoral process, political pluralism and participation, and functioning of government. The index evaluates human rights through the sub-categories freedom of expression and belief, associational and organizational rights, and personal autonomy and individual rights.[55] These measures of participation and human rights make up over fifty percent of the Freedom House's ranking system.

The Polity IV index assesses participation through their governance dimension. They measure participation with the category political legitimacy and the sub-categories of regime inclusions, factionalism, and political salience of elite ethnicity, polity fragmentation, and exclusionary ideology of ruling elite. The Polity index assesses human rights marginally with ethnic group political discrimination under the category of political legitimacy and state repression under the category of security legitimacy.

The Worldwide Governance Research Indicators Dataset (WGI) ranks states participation through the category voice and accountability but does not address human rights.[56] The Global Governance Initiative (GGI) does not assess participation but addresses human rights.[57] The World Governance Assessment (WGA) assesses both participation and human rights through its categories of political society and civil society respectively.[58] The African Governance Report (AGR) assesses participation and human rights through its categories of political governance and human rights.[59] This index groups human rights and rule of law together.[60] The Index of African Governance (IAG) assesses participation and human rights through its sub-categories of participation in elections and respect for civil and political rights.[61] The final index, the FSI assesses participation with the variables group grievance, factionalized elites, and legitimacy of the state. This index directly assesses human rights with the variable human rights.[62]

In conclusion, all indices assess the category of participation and human rights. However, two indices assess this category marginally by only look at one of the two aspects of participation and human rights. Six of the eight indices address both categories in a robust manner (see Table 10).

Table 10: Index treatment of participation and human rights.

	Participation	Human Rights	
FIW	Y	Y	
Polity	Y	Y	
WGI	Y	N	Source: Data based on author's evaluation of listed indices.
GGI	N	Y	
WGA	Y	Y	
AGR	Y	Y	
IAG	Y	Y	
FSI	Y	Y	

Human Development

Citizens charge their governments to supply the public good of effective human development. Citizens have rights to educational opportunity, health care, sanitary services, and poverty mitigation. Governments may provide these opportunities in a variety of ways – directly by the state in some countries, or by state-regulated agencies in others. However, regardless of the means by which these opportunities are provided, governments have a responsibility to provide for minimal standards in terms of outcomes.[63] Only four indices address this aspect of governance: Polity IV, the Global Governance Initiative (GGI), the Index of African Governance (IAG), and the Failed States Index (FSI).

The Polity IV Index addresses human development as a subcategory under their development dimension. The Polity index also assesses the human development component indirectly by measuring infant mortality. The GGI assesses human development through its categories of poverty and hunger, health, and education. The IAG assigns an entire category to human development. This category looks at poverty, health and sanitation, and education. Finally, the FSI assesses human development through the variables mounting demographic pressure and public services. Less than half of the indices address human development.

Economic Development

Economic development is the public good in which well-governed states create an environment which enables their citizens the opportunity to prosper. The state does so by providing regulatory frameworks conducive to creation of prosperity and also by creating stable and forward looking monetary and fiscal policy environments that facilitate and encourage national and personal wealth creation. Arteries of commerce – a robust physical communications and transportation infrastructure – are also critical to achieve these objectives. Many indices include environmental consideration as part of their ranking on economic development. The premise associated with the inclusion of environmental considerations is related to sustaining economic opportunity and human development over the long term.[64] Five of the eight indices rank states according to economic development: the Polity IV index, the World Governance Assessment (WGA), the African Governance

Report (AGR), the Index of African Governance (IAG), and the Failed States Index (FSI). The Global Governance Initiative (GGI) also looks at economic development but only in a narrow fashion assessing only environment sustainability and global partnerships.

The Polity index assesses economic development through two measures. The first measure is economic effectiveness measured by GDP per capita. The second is economic legitimacy measured by the percentage of export trade in manufactured goods. The WGA lists economic society as one of its specific categories. The AGR assesses economic development along two categories: economic governance and public financial management and private sector development and corporate governance. The IAG looks at economic development with a category classified as sustainable economic opportunity. It measures factors related to wealth creation, macroeconomic stability and financial integrity, the arteries of commerce, and environmental sensitivity. Finally, the FSI looks at uneven development and economic decline as measures of economic development.[65]

Rule of Law

This paper defines rule of law as a system in which laws are public knowledge and apply equally to everyone. Governments cannot function without rule of law. Rule of law refers not only to the Anglo-Saxon common law, the Napoleonic Code, Islamic jurisprudential methods, or others, but rather to any codified, transparent method of adjudicating personal disputes, formal and informal contractual obligation, and disputes between citizens and the state, without resort to violence. Thus, this category looks at the existence of enforceable codes of law and judicial mechanisms free of state control.[66] In addition, this category looks at the right to a fair and prompt hearing, and the presumption of innocence until proven guilty. Rule of law highlights the idea of laws enacted, laid down, and legislated by an authoritative body. Some authors use the term to highlight human rights and democracy; the idea of a universal higher law.[67] This broader second approach is addressed in the category of participation and human rights. Five of the eight indices address the category of rule of law. These indices are Freedom in the World (FIW), Worldwide Governance Research Indicators (WGI), World Governance Assessment (WGA), the African Governance Report (AGR), and the Index of African Governance (IAG).

FIW assesses rule of law as a subcategory within civil liberties. The WGI devotes an entire category of their ranking system to rule of law and also looks at control of corruption, regulatory quality, and government effectiveness. The AGR evaluates rule of law as part of its assessment of human rights.[68] In addition, the AGR assesses institutional checks and balances and institutional effectiveness and accountability of the executive to broaden its evaluation of rule of law. The IAG, like the WGI, devotes an entire category to rule of law. It subdivides this category into ratification of critical legal norms, judicial independence and efficiency, and corruption. The WGA looks at the judiciary, bureaucracy, and government from a rule of law perspective.[69]

Safety and Security

The final category of public goods supplied through good governance is that of safety and security; without which, good governance and the provision of all other public goods is impossible. War or ongoing insurgencies create conditions in which the citizens are neither safe nor secure. In addition, citizens of a modern state are not safe or secure if the government does not have mechanisms to provide for personal safety. Citizens demand to be free of mugging, carjacking, theft, rape, and homicide. Thus, personal safety is the second major component of the public good of safety and security.[70] Only five of the eight indices address this aspect of governance. Three of those five only address security narrowly (the Polity IV index, the Worldwide Governance Indicators (WGI), and the Global Governance Initiative (GGI)). The remaining two which assess security in a more robust manner are the Index of African Governance (IAG) and the Failed State Index (FSI).

The Polity IV index assesses security through security effectiveness measured by total residual war and political effectiveness defined as regime stability. This provides an adequate treatment of external threats and the internal threat of civil war or insurgency but completely neglects the safety aspect of this category and is thus incomplete. Similarly, the WGI only assesses safety and security as it relates to regime stability. The GGI's category of peace and security does not address the domestic concerns of crime and violence associated with safety.

Table 11: Index treatment of safety and security.

	Safety	Security	
FIW	N	N	
Polity	N	Y	
WGI	Marginal	Marginal	Source: Data based on author's evaluation of listed indices.
GGI	N	Y	
WGA	N	N	
AGR	N	N	
IAG	Y	Y	
FSI	Y	Y	

Of the indices that robustly evaluate safety and security, the IAG assesses both national security and public safety. The FSI addresses security obliquely through several variables: security apparatus, external intervention, refugees, and chronic or sustained human flight (see Table 11).[71]

Other Models

Several models of governance exist which look at governance and the roles of the state but do not rank states. The first of which is the Collier-Hoeffler model (CH). This model looks at variables related to the onset of civil war. The CH model uses greed, grievance, and opportunity as the driving causality factors for civil war. These factors can also assess state fragility. Greed under the CH construct can be thought of as an opposition group attempting to gain the resources of the state for their own ends. Grievance includes such factors as economic or land inequality and religious or ethnic marginalization in the political process. The third factor, opportunity, includes economic and educational factors, recent history of wars, and terrain factors. The CH model found the statistically significant variables included primary commodity as a percent of GDP, male secondary education, GDP growth, and time since the last war, geographic dispersion of the population, size of the country, social fractionalization, and ethnic dominance.[72] These final variables fit within the previously delineated categories of public goods delivered by the state to its citizens. The variables social fractionalization and ethnic dominance address participation but neglect human rights. The variable male secondary education addresses human development. The variables primary commodity as a percent of GDP and GDP growth address economic development. The variable time since last war partially addresses the category of safety and security while neglecting rule of law.

Table 12: Collier-Hoeffler Model.

Category of Public Goods	Collier –Hoeffler Model	
Participation and Human Rights	Social fractionalization	
	Ethnic Dominance	
Human Development	Male secondary education	
Economic Development	GDP growth	
	Primary commodity (% GDP)	
Rule of Law	Not addressed	
Safety and Security	Time since the last war	
Misc	Geographic dispersion of the population	
	Size of the country	

Source: Author's interpretation and categorization of the Collier-Hoeffler model.[73]

The next organization which looks at the roles of a state but does not provide an index is the Institute for State Effectiveness (ISE). US efforts in Afghanistan spurred the creation of the ISE.[74] It sub-divides a government's roles and responsibilities into ten categories grouped in three areas: economic, security, and government.[75] Under the economic grouping reside the roles of management of public finances, and regulation and oversight of the market. Under the security grouping ISE delineates the responsibilities of maintaining a monopoly on the means of violence and upholding the rule of law through police and judicial systems. Under the governmental grouping, ISE delineates the role of controlling the public administration, investing in human capital, running effective infrastructure services, investing in natural, industrial, and intellectual assets, defining the social contract, delineating the citizen's rights and duties, and oversight of international relations and public borrowing.[76] These roles also fit into the previously delineated categories. The definition of the social contract and delineation of the citizen's rights and duties address participation and human rights. Investment in human capital addresses the category human development. The ISE addresses economic development in a robust manner with a majority of the states roles falling into that category. Those roles include infrastructure, investing in natural, industrial, and intellectual assets, and oversight of public borrowing, management of public finances, and regulation and oversight of the market. Finally, the ISE addresses both rule of law and safety and security directly.

In conclusion, each ranking system discussed in the preceding sections espouses a much larger role for the state than the core role of safety and security. The manner in which the ranking systems structure their evaluation of state performance biases their results to overly reward performance in the category of participation and human rights. However, on the opposite end of the spectrum, only two completely address safety and security (Index of African Governance (IAG), and the Failed States Index (FSI)). Looking across the spectrum of governance, three of the indices offer a robust view, the Polity IV index, the

Table 13: Institution for State Effectiveness.

Category of Public Goods	Institute for State Effectiveness	
Participation and Human Rights	Define social contract and delineate rights and duties of citizens	
Human Development	Invest in human capital (health and education)	
Economic Development	Management of public finances	
	Regulation and oversight of the market	
	Run effective infrastructure services	
	Invest in natural, industrial, and intellectual assets	
	Oversee international relations and public borrowing	
Rule of Law	Uphold the rule of law	
	Control of the public administration	
Safety and Security	Monopoly on the means of violence	

Source: Author's interpretation and categorization of the Institute for State Effectiveness construct.[77]

IAG, and the FSI. The Polity IV index addresses all categories with the exception of rule of law but only marginally covers safety and security. The FSI also addresses all aspects of governance but neglects rule of law. As such, the IAG is the most complete ranking system. Common to all the indices is a methodological flaw which weighs each category equally. This equal weighting of state roles offers no insight into importance or prioritization. In a resource constrained environment, it is impossible and unrealistic to expect a state to pursue progress along all five categories simultaneously. An appropriate analogy for state roles which shows importance and priority is Maslow's hierarchy of needs (see Figure 2).

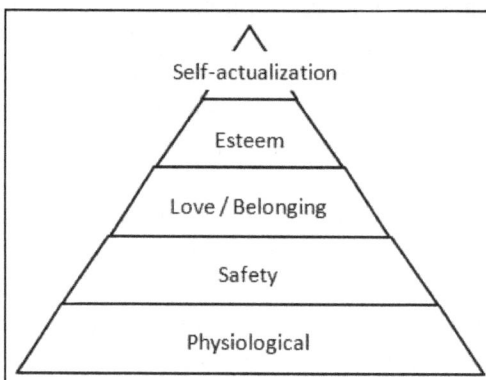

Figure 2: Maslow's hierarchy of needs.[78]

Maslow's hierarchy is a framework for human needs. His premise is that certain needs are more important than others and until the lower needs are met, the individual cannot pursue higher needs. To reach a higher level, one must first achieve all the previous needs. The top levels of Maslow's hierarchy of needs are self-actualization and esteem. Self actualization is associated with achieving a person's full potential. Maslow describes this desire as the desire to become everything that one is capable of becoming.[79] Self actualization is equivalent to the state role of participation. Through participation in the political process, citizens shape their future in order to achieve their full potential and become self-actualized. A failed state is not one which fails to allow its citizens to realize their true potential. That state is progressing with regards to state roles lower and more basic on the hierarchy of state roles. It must set the conditions at lower levels prior to pursuing roles at the apex of the pyramid. Defining good governance as equivalent to good political governance is too narrow. It ignores the central responsibility of a state to provide safety and security for its citizens.[80]

Participation can in some respect run contrary to the other roles of the state such as safety and security in the case of ethnic violence by the democratically elected majority. "Suppose the election was declared free and fair" but those elected are "racists, fascists, separatists, who are publicly opposed to [peace and reintegration]."[81] Participation can also run contrary to rule of law in the case of partiality in the courts based on ethnicity. It can work against economic development with redistribution of property dictated by the majority. Participation can even sabotage human rights through minority repression.

The next level of Maslow's hierarchy of needs concerns esteem. Esteem is the normal human desire for others to be valued and accepted. Esteem is comparable to the state role regarding human rights. The expectations and definition of human rights vary between countries and cultures. A prominent example of this ongoing conflict is between the UN Declaration of Human Rights and the Cairo Declaration of Human Rights. The Cairo Declaration clearly indicates the subordination of human rights as defined by the UN to *Sharia* law. Thus ranking and evaluating state performance based on a Western interpretation of human rights is not a valid assessment tool. The "problems of precipitous liberalization often outweigh the benefits and … contribute greatly to great [state] fragility."[82] Many states in the developing world are not ready for a modern, liberal democracy based on their underlying culture and religious values. Early adoption of western forms of government due to international pressure may cause more instability versus stability.

At the opposite end of the spectrum, Maslow places physiological needs and safety at the bottom of his pyramid. Physiological needs include basics such as water, food, and air. Individuals can obtain these requirements from the global commons as long as there is rule of law to give order to human interactions. The next level of safety takes precedence over all other needs and will dominate individual behavior. This need corresponds to the state role of safety and security and flows from the philosophical definition of the role of the state; the "state is a human community that (successfully) claims the monopoly of the legitimate use of physical force within a given territory."[83] A state that cannot provide rule of law, safety and security for its citizens cannot and should not concentrate on any other task until it can do so. These needs of safety and security and rule of law are the foundation upon which all other state roles are built.

All the indices measure achievement of modern, western, democratic forms of government and do not acknowledge that the state must structure the delivery of public goods in a sequential and hierarchical basis with safety and security and rule of law providing a foundation upon which the state builds delivery of all other public goods. These indices emphasize higher end roles such as participation and human rights, neglect safety and security, and skew the results of their analysis. Safety and security is the core role of the state and the role that must be pursued first. Under this construct authoritarian governments are acceptable as long as they provide for the physical security of their citizenry. These authoritarian regimes will progress over time as their citizens demand higher public goods on the hierarchy of state roles once the foundational roles of safety and security are met.

The time required for state progression up the pyramid of state roles is measured in decades not years. A relevant example is the slow growth of modern Western democracies across history. The British king signed the Magna Carta in 1215 marking the initiation of liberalization and democracy in the West which culminated in the adoption of the US Constitution in 1787 a time period of 572 years. In 1789, the French Revolution and its liberal ideals actually led to greater instability not more stability. The new French state only stabilized with the Third Republic in 1870, a period of 81 years. In both cases these western countries had hundreds of years to consolidate a sense of identity, nationalism, and borders. The developing world does not have these advantages due to artificial borders, lack of shared history, and mixed ethnicities. Thus, democracy would take even longer to consolidate and grow within the developing world.

A more modern example of the time required for a state to progress along the pyramid of needs is women's voting rights in the United States. In the United States, a nation founded upon the ideals of participation and human rights, it took 144 years to give women the right to vote by passing the 19th Amendment in 1920. To expect a developing country, struggling with other aspects of governance and does not have the same liberal historical background as the United States, to immediately give women voting rights or allow full political participation is unrealistic. Both state roles of participation and human rights are at the apex of Maslow's pyramid, important but only if all lower needs are met.

An appropriate construct for applying time to the progression of state roles is the concept of organic governments. Governments must grow in the context of a people's organic culture, values, and beliefs over time. The above indices and ranking systems look too broadly at the modern trapping of our mature liberal democracies. Any government which grows organically from its root culture, according to the traditions, values, and beliefs of that culture, will necessarily first satisfy the foundation of Maslow's pyramid by providing safety and security for its citizenry. An organic government which does not provide that critical public good will quickly be overthrown and replaced.[84]

This monograph proposes a hierarchy of state roles parallel to Maslow's hierarchy of needs in which the state pursues the roles of governance in a sequential and hierarchical basis with safety and security and rule of law providing a foundation upon which the state builds delivery of all other public goods. Safety and security with rule of law form the foundation of the pyramid while participation and human rights form the apex of the pyramid. Human and economic development occupies the middle ground.

Self-actualization

Participation and Human Rights

Esteem

Human Development

Love / Belonging

Economic Development

Safety

Rule of Law

Physiological

Safety and Security

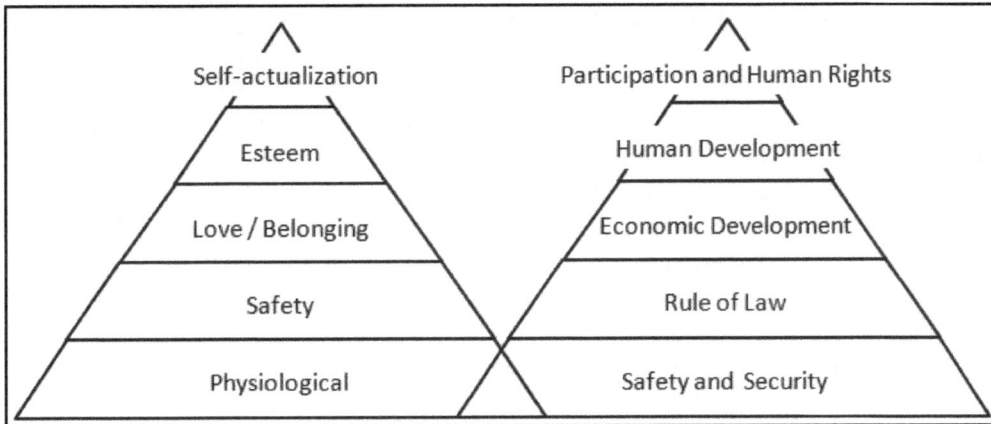

Figure 3: State role hierarchy.[85]

The Index of African Governance (IAG) illustrates the value of this construct. It is the most robust of all the discussed indices and addresses all five categories of public goods. When one looks at the top ten countries as ranked by the IAG, four of the overall top ten actually fall within the bottom half of the African continent when evaluated for safety and security. The most glaring examples of this mismatch are South Africa and Botswana, ranked forty-eighth and thirty-seventh out of fifty-three states for safety and security. Given the importance of safety and security to effective governance, this represents a nearly fifty percent error margin due to the lack of a hierarchical construct for state functions. Thus, these indices do not accurately evaluate good governance unless they view the roles of a state in a sequential or hierarchical basis. The true definition of a failed state is failure to claim a monopoly on the legitimate use of physical force within a given territory.

Applying the New Understanding of State to the Mexican Case

Mexico's stability is critically important to the United States. It possesses a GDP larger than twenty-two of our twenty-eight NATO allies[86] and also possesses the world's seventeenth largest oil reserves.[87] In addition, Mexico shares the US southern border making its success critical to US domestic interests. Much of the US ability to be involved in the international arena stems from the nature of our demilitarized borders with Mexico and Canada. During the Pershing Expedition, the United States utilized over 75,000 National Guard troops to secure the border with Mexico.[88] This border security mission engaged half of the US Army. Had the conflict continued, it could have diverted US participation in World War I. Imagine that scenario today with drug fueled violence causing a similar security situation and how border security would impact the already strained US military.

Of the eight previously discussed indices, there are five indices that evaluate Mexico: Freedom in the World (FIW), the Polity IV Index, the Worldwide Governance Research Indicators (WGI), the Global Governance Initiative (GGI), and the Failed State Index (FSI). The World Governance Assessment (WGA) only looks at sixteen selected countries, while the African Governance Report (AGR) and the Index of African Governance (IAG) are Africa specific.

Mexico ranks well in overall governance for each index. Freedom in the World ranks Mexico as free giving it high marks in both its subcategories of political rights and civil liberties.[89] Similarly, the Polity IV Index also gives Mexico a high score with a low fragility score of 3 out of 25.[90] The WGI gives Mexico a modest composite score of 46 out of 100[91] and the GGI ranks Mexico as on-track.[92] Finally, the FSI ranks Mexico as borderline (not stable and not in danger).[93] Thus, two of the five ranking systems rate Mexico in the upper quartile of state performance, while the other three rate Mexico in the middle quartiles, doing an average job of governance. None of the ranking systems rate Mexico in the lowest quartile, as a failed state. Figure 4 shows the overall rankings related to Mexico broken down into quartiles.

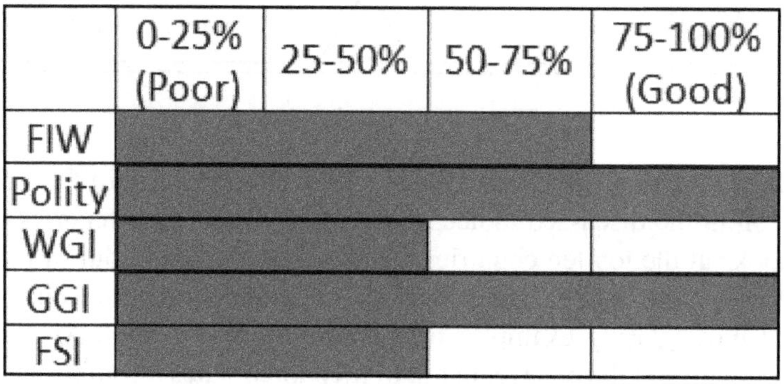

	0-25% (Poor)	25-50%	50-75%	75-100% (Good)
FIW				
Polity				
WGI				
GGI				
FSI				

Figure 4: Overall governance rankings for Mexico.[94]

Despite Mexico's solid performance, illustrated by these rankings systems, stories of catastrophe in Mexico continually inundate the news media. It seems the problems facing Mexico are insurmountable; from drug trafficking, violent and nonviolent crime, growing welfare, educational and medical costs, and racial strife, to economic losses for US investors, companies, and labor, and concerns about illegal immigration. Mexico is in dire straits according to the news. The following sections will take a more detailed look at the performance of Mexico with regards to the delivery of public goods along the five categories.

Participation and Human Rights

Mexico is doing well with respect to the delivery of the public good of participation and human rights. All of the five indices assess the category of participation and human rights in Mexico. Freedom in the World (FIW) gives Mexico a score of 2 for political rights and 3 for civil liberties on a seven point scale with seven representing poor delivery of participation and human rights. FIW rates Mexico as free.[95] The Polity IV index gives Mexico a yellow assessment (low fragility) for security legitimacy (state repression) and political legitimacy. This index classifies Mexico as a democratic regime.[96] The WGI only looks at participation but gives Mexico a moderate score of 50.5 out of 100 for voice and accountability.[97]

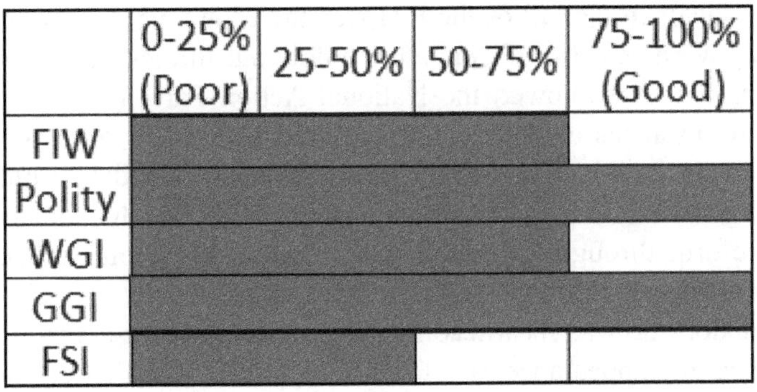

	0-25% (Poor)	25-50%	50-75%	75-100% (Good)
FIW	███	███	███	
Polity	███	███	███	███
WGI	███	███	███	
GGI	███	███	███	███
FSI	███	███		

Figure 5: Participation and human rights rankings for Mexico.[98]

The GGI only looks at women's rights but assesses that Mexico is on track for its category of gender equality and empowering women.[99] Finally, the FSI gives Mexico moderate scores of between five and six out of ten for the variables relating to participation and human rights (group grievances, factionalized elites, legitimacy of the state, and human rights).[100] Figure 5 shows the rankings for participation and human rights related to Mexico broken down into quartiles.

Mexico hasn't always performed well with respect to participation and human rights. The revolutionaries founded the Mexican Revolution on the principles of sovereignty, social justice, and democracy. The revolution itself was an assault on the people of Mexico, with casualties amounting to over ten percent of the entire population. The ideas of the revolution, sovereignty, social justice and democracy, were codified in the 1917 Constitution. However, these constitutional mechanisms were insufficient to keep these revolutionary promises to the citizens of Mexico.

From a participation perspective, Mexican history is not one of an ideal liberal democracy. In fact, the "perfect dictatorship is not communism, not the Soviet Union, not Cuba, but Mexico, because it is a camouflaged dictatorship."[101] This quotation refers to the iron fisted rule of the Institutional Revolutionary Party (PRI). The PRI survived as the sole source of political power in Mexico for seventy-one years since its inception in 1929. It did this through a unique system of noncompetitive elections within a formally multiparty, pluralistic system and a president vested with quasi-monarchical powers. In addition, the all powerful president could hand pick his successor within the one-party PRI system thus diluting the constitutional limit to presidential power of only one six-year term.

The PRI maintained its power through cooptation and intimidation. Cooptation is the process by which the ruling party trades small concessions or favors to individuals or groups which are independent enough to threaten the ongoing domination of the ruling party in exchange for a moderation of their demands and a reduction in their challenge to the dominant group's control over the system.[102] The PRI utilized cooptation to incorporate revolutionary aspects into the prevailing order. In essence, the PRI bought off the opposition and rolled them into the existing PRI structure. If the PRI was unable to co-opt opposing elements, the regime would use force to remove the opposition from the picture. The Mexican press referred to this process of cooptation as 'pan o palo' bread or the stick[103].

A massive factor in the fall of the PRI was the economic decline in the 1980s which prevented the government from being able to dole out further payments to co-opt or buy the opposition. The PRI allowed the National Action Party (PAN) to run in elections. Early on, many instances of voter fraud occurred which led to a widespread feeling of disenfranchisement culminating in the president being jeered in front of a worldwide audience during the World Cup soccer play-offs in 1986.[104] This incident spurred further promises of reform through the creation of a watchdog group called the Democratic Assembly for Effective Suffrage. However, the assassination of a close Cardenas aide, Francisco Ovando, who was spearheading the drive to place observers in Mexico's polling stations, crushed any appearance of reform.[105] The PRI won that election but at the cost of discrediting the entire PRI system of power. The only way forward was for PRI to utilize a genuinely pluralistic system. The electoral crisis forced the PRI to reestablish their legitimacy through establishing effective suffrage. PAN, utilizing this window, built on piecemeal gubernatorial and municipality victories and gained control of Congress in 1997 and the presidency in 2000.

Today, Mexico has moved away from an authoritarian, repressive, hegemonic, non-competitive, elite dominated and opaque political system towards liberal democratic values and practices.[106] Previously, there was no way for the opposition to air their views in an effective, constitutional means without resorting to violence and revolution. Now Mexico has true political participation in free elections with both Dahl's aspects of 'polyarchy' – contestation and participation.[107]

From a human rights perspective, the PRI was not particularly enthusiastic about the promotion of human rights.[108] The 1917 Constitution enshrined a set of individual guarantees for the protection of civil and political rights as well as social rights such as education, access to land, housing, and health. However, the procedural mechanisms available to protect and enforce these rights were inadequate.[109] PRI rule often involved systematic and grave violation of human rights.[110] A stunning example of which is the 1968 Tlatelolco massacre where troops opened fire on several hundred student protestors in advance of the Olympic Games. This massacre left a huge scar upon the Mexican psyche.

The final straw contributing to the downfall of the PRI came with the Mexican government's handling of the 1994 indigenous peasant rebellion championed by the Zapatista Army of National Liberation (EZLN) in Chiapas. The government responded with a heavy military hand resulting in severe violations of human rights. Local non-governmental organizations (NGOs) estimated that there were 12,000 individual displaced persons (IDPs) and hundreds of violent deaths.[111] This incident generated massive international pressure on the Mexican government; "the events that have taken place in Chiapas since 1994 put in the spotlight an undeniable and intolerable truth [of human rights violations] which had been ignored by society and the government."[112]

President Carlos Salinas implemented an explicit human rights policy through the creation of the National Commission on Human Rights (CNDH).[113] Following Salinas, presidents Zedillo and Fox continued expanding governmental awareness and responsiveness to human rights violations. They opened Mexico to international monitoring and assistance and continued constitutional and legal reforms to include the creation of a Special Prosecutor's Office for Social and Political Movements of the Past "to investigate and prosecute past abuses committed against dissidents and opposition groups by state security forces."[114] Mexico is now upholding the constitutional guarantee of a free press, investigating and rectifying past human rights abuses.[115] In conclusion, although Mexico has a troubled history with respect to participation and human rights, Mexico is doing a good job in the delivery of the public good of participation and human rights to its citizens.

Human Development

Overall, Mexico is doing well with respect to the delivery of the public good of human development. Three of the five indices discussed above look at the category of human development for Mexico. The Polity IV index gives Mexico a green assessment (no fragility) for social effectiveness and legitimacy.[116] The GGI assesses that Mexico has achieved the Millennium Challenge goals associated with education and is on track to achieve the goals associated with poverty and hunger. In the category of health, Mexico has achieved child health goals and is on track to achieve the goals associated with combating HIV, malaria, and other diseases. With regards to the goals related to maternal health it is possible for Mexico to achieve these goals if a few changes are made.[117] Finally, the FSI gives moderate scores of between six and seven to Mexico for the variables relating to human development (demographic pressures and public services).[118] Figure 6 shows the rankings for human development related to Mexico broken down into quartiles.

	0-25% (Poor)	25-50%	50-75%	75-100% (Good)
FIW	N/A			
Polity				
WGI	N/A			
GGI				
FSI				

Figure 6: Human development rankings for Mexico.[119]

Mexico has not always done well with respect to human development. From a historical perspective, Mexico's greatest challenge relates to meeting the needs of the rural poor. One of the original driving forces behind the Mexican Revolution was the needs of the landless peasants.[120] The modern Zapatista revolution in Chiapas draws its roots from those same challenges. The Chiapas region is rich in resources but contains the poorest people in Mexico. It has fertile soil, good rain, leads the country in hydro power, and is third in petroleum exports. Unfortunately, the Mexican government focused their efforts with respect to human development in the northern urban areas.

Expanding services related to human development is a difficult task since Mexico consists of a wide and scarcely integrated territory of almost two million square kilometers, poor communication systems, a fast growing population, and the existence of indigenous groups in isolated areas. The scope of the problem of human development in Mexico is impressive. Today, the Mexican education system serves over thirty million students, 1.6 million teachers, and more than 229,000 schools.[121] Despite these challenges, the Mexican government has done an incredible job. This section will specifically look at education as indicative of progress throughout the spectrum of human development.

Between 1970 and 2000, Mexico significantly expanded basic education services. Enrollment has more than doubled from 9.7 million students to 21.6 million. This increase in educational services was greater than the associated population increase resulting in an enrollment rate increase from 70 to 88 percent.[122] Another example of educational improvement in Mexico is an increase in attainment level. In 1993, the average educational attainment level was 6.8 years which increased to 7.9 years in 2003. These dramatic increases in enrollment and attainment were due to increased public spending. From 1995 to 2001, public spending on basic education in Mexico increased by 36 percent.[123] Education is the largest component of public spending of the Mexican government (24 percent of programmable spending in 2003). In fact, since 1996, investment in the Mexican education system increased at a higher rate than GDP growth.[124]

In addition to the progress noted above, the government of Mexico created four major programs to further improve the education system in Mexico. *Oportunidades* (formerly known as PROGRESA) provides cash grants to low-income families so that their children can attend school and receive health services. *Enciclomedia* digitalizes the school curriculum into CD-ROMs so students can learn interactively with the aid of computers. *Programa Escuelas de Calidad*, or quality schools program, targets low performing schools. Targeted schools must consent to implement a school wide reform project; in exchange, they receive grants of up to $10,000 to be used mainly for infrastructure improvements.[125] In conclusion, although Mexico challenges with respect to human development, Mexico is doing well in the delivery of the public good of human development.

Economic Development

In conjunction with human development, Mexico is performing well with respect to the delivery of the public good of economic development. Two of the five indices discussed above examine economic development in Mexico. The Polity IV index gives Mexico a green assessment (no fragility) for economic effectiveness and legitimacy.[126] The FSI gives Mexico moderate scores of between six and eight for the variables relating to economic development (uneven development and economic decline).[127] Figure 7 shows the rankings for economic development related to Mexico broken down into quartiles.

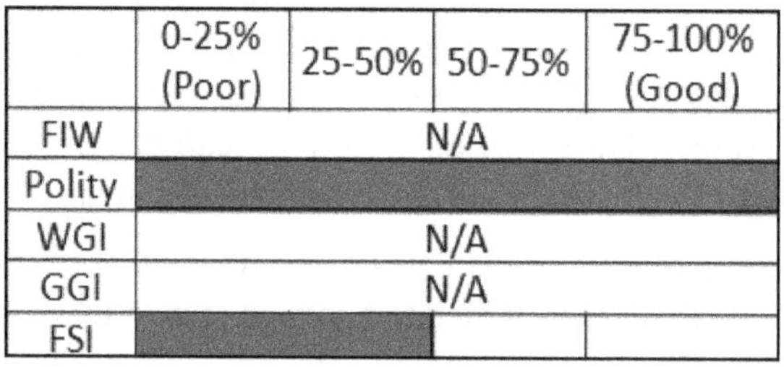

	0-25% (Poor)	25-50%	50-75%	75-100% (Good)
FIW	N/A			
Polity				
WGI	N/A			
GGI	N/A			
FSI				

Figure 7: Economic development rankings for Mexico.[128]

36

From a historical perspective, Mexico has traveled a long rocky road on the path to economic development. During World War II, Mexico was a vital supplier of raw materials and labor. The Mexican government used this capital as a seed for economic expansion under the concept of import substitution. This concept builds and protects local manufacturing industries in order to gradually replace foreign imports with domestically produced products. The Mexican government used tariffs to insulate the nascent Mexican industries from foreign competition. Initially, this concept did a great job at stimulating the Mexican economy and resulted in the Mexican economic 'miracle' of the 1960s.

However, this concept of import substitution has inherent limitations. In theory, the government protects the infant industries until they mature to a stage at which they can compete on the international market. In practice, since they developed in an environment with no competition, those protected industries never developed the efficiencies and productivity to allow effective competition on the open international market.

President Echeverria tried to rejuvenate the concept of import substitution in the 1970s with the hope of reviving the Mexican miracle. He initiated massive state-sponsored investment used to create a second stage of industrialization. However, the state, not economic criteria, dictated the selection and execution of projects. In addition, Mexico drew heavily on foreign loans to fund this second wave of industrialization. Simultaneously, the Echeverria administration increased spending on social programs including housing, health, social security, education, and transportation.[129] This two-pronged expansion of government created a massive deficit accompanied by rampant inflation and initiated a massive recession.

During this recession, Mexico completely depleted its international reserves and could not make payments on its foreign debt. Pressure from the international community forced Echeverria's successor, President Portillo, to declare bankruptcy. He subsequently blamed the economic collapse on the financial sector but governmental decisions related to over spending on social programs and state-led industrialization actually led to the crash. Due to the disastrous economic policies of his predecessors, President Madrid (1982-1988) was left with debt equal to two-thirds of Mexico's GDP.[130] The International Monetary Fund dictated that the administration slash its budget deficit from 18 to 3.5 percent of GDP. To accomplish this goal, the Madrid administration instituted an austerity program by cutting governmental spending related to social programs and reducing the size of the bureaucracy. These actions hurt the Mexican citizen and were economically disastrous due to the high degree of state involvement in the economy. The economic decline affected every citizen as inflation rose to 160 percent by 1987.[131] The average Mexican worker lost forty to fifty percent of his purchasing power. Per capita GDP fell from 3170 US dollars in 1981 to 1860 US dollars in 1988.[132]

Despite the bleak economic outlook, these dire events were the genesis of long-term recovery. The mental paradigm of the Mexican leadership changed and "concluded that further growth, employment creation, and great efficiency cannot be achieved through continued expansion of the public sector. Rather, progress must come from a reinvigorated private sector, one more fully integrated with the international economy."[133] The administration reversed the number of state owned corporations or *parastatals*.[134] In many cases these *parastatals* were operating at a loss or severely indebted. The administration could absorb the debt or simply liquidate the asset. Liquidation created a second order effect of additional unemployed workers.

The final, sustained recovery came about through the North American Free Trade Agreement (NAFTA) and the rise of *maquiladora* plants across Mexico.[135] The *maquiladora* eventually gained parity with tourism as the second largest source of foreign exchange for Mexico. The US Congress ratified NAFTA in 1994. [136] NAFTA represented international recognition that Mexico's socioeconomic and political positions were sufficiently stable to be worthy of such an important economic integration.[137] Since the passage of NAFTA, trade within the region doubled over the period of 1994 to 2007 to a high of $621 billion. Foreign direct investment also doubled to $299 billion.[138] NAFTA is the world's largest free trade area encompassing one-third of the world's total GDP – significantly larger than the EU.[139] Specific to Mexico, imports have also doubled from $51.1 billion to $107.2 billion and exports to the United States grew over 200 percent while exports to Canada more than tripled.

This rosy economic picture is countered by many experts stating that GDP growth per capita has been low and even negative at times after the passage of NAFTA.[140] Mexican labor force growth explains this anomaly. Mexico has a traditionally high birth rate. In addition, a growing number of women entered the labor force during this period.[141] This labor force growth is independent of NAFTA. The economic benefits of NAFTA are offsetting what would otherwise be a catastrophic problem for Mexico.

In summary, the Mexican economy is healthy. Mexican exports are expanding, wages are increasing, poverty is decreasing, and foreign investment is increasing.[142] In addition, as an argument in support of the hierarchy of state roles, NAFTA positively affected political change within Mexico and resulted in a level of governmental responsiveness and accountability seldom seen in Mexican history.[143] However, "free trade alone is not enough." The benefits of free trade will continue to be sub-optimal "without significant policy and institutional reforms."[144]   Stephen Johnson also notes, "initial efforts at … replacing import substitution practices with open markets and free trade, privatizing inefficient state industries, and introducing solid macroeconomic fundamentals will reach a point of diminishing returns absent the further development of confidence inspiring public institutions and the rule of law."[145]

Rule of Law

Mexico is doing poorly with respect to the delivery of the public good of rule of law. A national survey estimates that Mexicans spend $1.6 billion on bribes each year. This involves an estimated 100 million corrupt transactions by Mexican citizens to obtain public services.[146] In addition to reports of rampant corruption, law enforcement and the judicial system are unable to reign in the drug cartels. "In Mexico … crime is a career option that competes with others."[147]

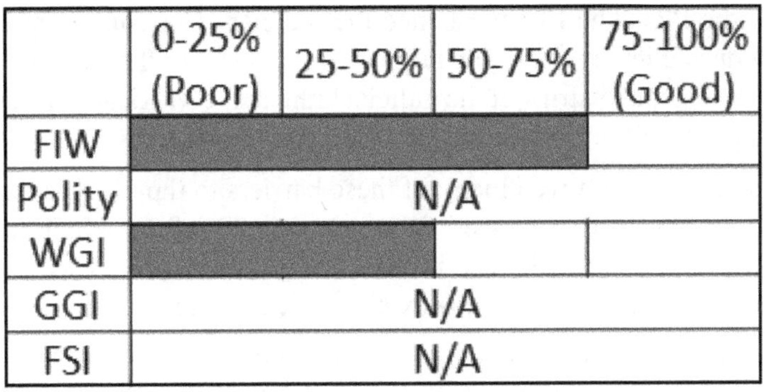

	0-25% (Poor)	25-50%	50-75%	75-100% (Good)
FIW	▓	▓	▓	
Polity	N/A			
WGI	▓	▓		
GGI	N/A			
FSI	N/A			

Figure 8: Rule of law rankings for Mexico.[148]

Two of the five indices discussed above look at the category of rule of law for Mexico. Freedom in the World gives Mexico a score of 3 for civil liberties on a scale of 1-7 (1 being the highest and 7 being the lowest). The civil liberties category includes a sub-category of rule of law.[149] The WGI looks at rule of law and corruption. It gives Mexico a score of 29.7 and 49.8 respectively (with 100 being a perfect score).[150] Both of these rankings give a false report in light of the shocking amount of capital that Mexican citizen must invest in bribes and the inability of the judicial system to affect the drug cartels. Figure 8 shows the rankings for rule of law related to Mexico broken down into quartiles.

Corruption in Mexico is an ingrained social institution whose origins trace to colonial times.[151] The revolution recognized this legacy of corruption inherited from Spanish colonialism and crafted the constitution to provide rule of law and protect against corruption. Article 17 of the Mexican Constitution requires prompt, complete, impartial, and gratuitous impartation of justice. Article 14 of the Mexican Constitution guarantees individual citizens the right to defend their life, liberty, property, and possessions by means of trial in an established tribunal with a public defender if needed.[152] However, until 2008 there was no presumption of innocence in the Mexican legal system.[153] In addition, there are no trails by jury. In the majority of cases, there are also no oral arguments, meaning lawyers do not stand in front of a judge to plead their client's case. Judges usually never meet the accused and cases are arbitrated through paperwork. As a final difference from a US conception of justice, judges are not given the latitude to decide the merits of a case but are subject to a Napoleonic code of justice where the laws are strictly codified; leaving judges little room for judgment.[154]

Despite the differences, there is a codified legal system in Mexico. However, legal proceedings in Mexico are often inefficient and uncertain. The Mexican public perceives that the "contravention of the law is the daily rule rather than the exception."[155] The judicial system is one in which access to justice is circumscribed along urban-rural and wealth-poverty lines[156] or loosely correlated with skin tone and social class.[157] Often the public views the Mexican judicial system as an instrument of the elite for subjugating the poor and uneducated.

A partial explanation for this lack of strength within the judicial branch of government comes from the legacy of PRI rule. A strong judiciary threatened the continued political dominance of the PRI. The PRI weakened the judiciary to ensure control of the political establishment during its seven decade reign.[158] As a result of the executive branch's power coupled with its fear and distrust of the judicial branch, the Mexican Supreme Court (SCJN) spent the better part of the twentieth century passively watching.[159]

The fall of the PRI removed many of these barriers to the exercise of judicial powers. President Zedillo (1994-2000) passed sweeping judicial reform which finally allowed the SCJN the effective power and freedom to rule against the interests of the executive.[160] Despite these sweeping changes, the Mexican judicial system is still failing.

Current statistics related to the rule of law in Mexico are shocking. Someone committing a crime in Mexico has only a two in 100 chance of getting caught and punished.[161] Of those suspected criminals caught by police officials, in nine of ten cases, suspects were found guilty without any scientific evidence like fingerprints or DNA.[162] In more than six of every ten cases, officials arrested suspects within three hours of the crime, leaving little time for serious detective work. Almost none were shown an arrest warrant. Once arrested, officials process only one in ten in accordance with the requirements of the law.[163] Once jailed, approximately 42 percent of Mexico's inmates languish in jail without ever having faced trial.[164] A suspected indigenous criminal faces an even worse situation with pretrial detention longer than allowed by law for over seventy percent of the indigenous prisoners in Mexico.[165]

The current Mexican population understands the weakness of their judicial system.[166] Polls which measure the percent of the population with no confidence in the legal system show a dramatic increase over the years, from twelve percent in 1981 to 25 percent in 1997. This trend continues with 81 percent of Mexican citizens polled in 2002 having little or no confidence in the judicial branch of government.[167] President Zedillo remarked when embarking on his reforms of the judicial branch of government that "we do not have the rule of law that is required for Mexico to develop."[168] His reforms although well intentioned have still not brought about rule of law to Mexico. Mexico's legal system has stagnated and deteriorated with respect to the quality of judicial institutions, public confidence in judicial institutions, the delivery of judicial services, the protection of tangible and intellectual property rights, the amount of time required to enforce a contract and evict a tenant, judicial opacity, perception of law and order, and the overall strength of the rule of law. [169]

Mexico's failure to uphold the rule of law has far reaching developmental consequences. Rule of law and the economic arena are intimately linked. Mexican citizens already have a propensity to structure their personal and business affairs around informal or reputation based networks of familial or personal contacts, thereby precluding the formation of the more impersonal credit and transactional relationships that lie at the heart of dynamic markets.[170] Much of this reluctance is due to lack of faith in the judicial systems and rule of law. Thomas Hobbes also recognized this linkage between economic activity and rule of law; "he that performeth first has no assurance the other will perform after because the bonds of words are too weak to bridle men's ambitious, avarice, anger, and other passions without the fear of some coercive power."[171] Rule of law must precede economic development.

Safety and Security

In addition to poor performance in regards to rule of law, Mexico is doing poorly with respect to the delivery of the public good of safety and security. Four of the five indices rank safety and security for Mexico, three of which only assess a narrow definition of safety and security. The Polity IV index gives Mexico a yellow assessment (low fragility) for security effectiveness and classifies the country's level of armed conflict as war.[172] This assessment does not look at issues relating to safety. The WGI only looks at safety and security from the perspective of political stability or regime change but gives Mexico a low score of 24.4 (out of 100) for political stability.[173] The GGI looks at peace and security but only assesses that category as related to the entire international community. The UN does not report individual state progress towards this category.[174] Finally, the FSI, with a robust assessment, gives Mexico a moderate score of 4.3 related to refugees and internally displaced persons and poor scores of between six and seven for other variables related to safety and security such as security apparatus, external intervention, and human flight.[175] Figure 9 shows the rankings for safety and security related to Mexico broken down into quartiles.

	0-25% (Poor)	25-50%	50-75%	75-100% (Good)
FIW	N/A			
Polity	░░░	░░░	░░░	
WGI	░░░	░		
GGI	N/A			
FSI	░░░	░░░	░░░	

Figure 9: Safety and security rankings for Mexico.[176]

The current situation in Mexico regarding safety and security is so dire that the State Department issued a travel warning to US citizens advising them to avoid travel to Mexico.[177] This is due to a marked increase in crime including murder, rape, and kidnapping. Kidnapping is perhaps the most destabilizing form of crime in Mexico since it frequently involves official corruption. Over 90 percent of kidnappings in Mexico are not reported to police because many Mexicans feel the authorities are complicit in most kidnappings.[178] In addition to the crimes above, the lesser crimes of street mugging, residential and commercial burglaries, and auto thefts are also sharply on the rise because of police corruption. The police not only accept bribes to turn a blind eye, but are frequently the perpetrators. The current administration is attempting to combat police corruption as evidenced by the suspension of an entire police force of 550 officers for allegations that they were serving as escorts for planeloads of cocaine but the problems continue.[179]

While crime and corrupt police officials are a serious threat to safety and security for Mexico, the gravest threat is the rise of drug related violence. The drug cartels operating within Mexico are a two-pronged threat–they challenge the central control of the government and simultaneously undermine governmental institutions. The drug trade within Mexico corrupts everything it touches, especially institutions of government. Similar to the PRI's 'pan o palo' policy, the drug cartels within Mexico have a *'plata o plomo'* policy, the bribe or the bullet. The drug henchmen are the modern day caciques (strongmen) of the post-colonial era. The drug violence even has the potential to corrupt progress with regards to the public good of participation as drug families come into power through the ballot box and are seen as *campesino* – or new patrons for the poor.

For most of the 20th century, Mexico's ruling party, the PRI, oversaw a system of narco-corruption that brought stability to the drug trade.[180] Bribes from the cartels to officials kept violence at a minimum. The PRI protected the cartel leaders and resolved conflict between different cartels by playing the role of peacemaker and mediator. The PRI allocated drug corridors to each cartel, thus physically separating them to lessen drug related violence. As the referee of disputes, the PRI was a stabilizing mechanism and apparatus to control, contain, and protect those groups. However, the decline of the one party system led to the collapse of this central mediator. With no central governing authority, the cartels fell into a new Hobbesian struggle for control of the drug corridors. "If there is no referee, the cartels will have to resolve disputes themselves, and drug traffickers don't do this by having meetings."[181]

Each newly elected president since the fall of the PRI has included attacking the drug cartels operating within Mexico part of their presidential platform. When elected as the first non-PRI president in modern Mexican history, President Vicente Fox pledged to wage "the mother of all battles" against the narco-traficantes.[182] In response to the governmental crackdown, the cartels turned on the authorities by ambushing police convoys, executing well-coordinated attacks against isolated governmental outposts and murdering officials in charge of the design and prosecution of counter-narcotic operations. This violence continues to escalate today with 5,400 drug related slayings in 2008, more than double the 2,477 reported in 2007.[183] There is even speculation that the two lead cartels declared peace to focus on fighting the government.

A recent example of the violence occurred in February 2009. The lead anti-drug official for the Benito Juarez municipality was brutally killed after less than 24 hours on the job. When his body was found, he was shot 11 times. An autopsy later revealed severe burns and broken bones in his hands, knees, and wrists. His killers tortured him before his death.[184] The previous year contained other examples of high profile drug related violence with the assassination of the head of Mexico's federal police and the arrest of Mexico's top antidrug prosecutor for being on a cartel payroll.[185]

These dramatic examples illustrate the reach, scope, and brutality of the drug cartels and show that the cartels are well organized, well trained, and well equipped. The cartels have transitioned from gangsterism to paramilitary terrorism with guerilla tactics. Their tactics are to sow fear and demonstrate that the cartels are the dominant force in Mexico (not the government). The cartels are recruiting former military and police officials as well as common criminals.

The gold standard in cartel violence, training, and equipment is Los Zetas.[186] This organization started in 1997 from a core group of thirty-one Mexican Army Special Forces deserters from elite counter-narcotics units. The group now numbers in the hundreds and is able to execute very elaborate and advanced attacks. For example, in recent attacks they used cell phone signatures to coordinate assassinations and kidnappings.[187] Prior attacks also show that Los Zetas penetrated Mexican law enforcement radio frequencies and can conduct attacks at will with high powered weaponry such as grenade launchers, helicopters, improvised explosive devices, and .50 caliber machine guns.[188]

In conjunction with the cartels' campaign of violence, they are waging an information war by publishing lists of targeted officials, posting their execution videos, and coercing newspapers into providing graphic coverage of their deeds.[189] In cartel controlled regions, they are even setting up a parallel tax system which threatens to completely usurp the Mexican government's control.[190] Los Zetas promise good salary, food, and medical care for new recruits' families as well as loans and life insurance.[191] The cartels are the state in areas they control or a shadow government in contested areas.

On a positive note, this narco-violence does not doom Mexico to failure. Mexico is in a stronger position to fight and win this battle than much of Latin America since much of their country is not suitable for growing or smuggling drugs. In addition, the size of their economy ensures that drug money cannot become a dominant export as in Columbia, Bolivia, or Peru.

However, even as the Mexican government fights the cartels, the manner in which it conducts counter-drug operations places the state at even greater risk. The administration is utilizing the military instead of law enforcement organization for most drug operations due to concerns regarding corruption. Thus far these military actions have been extremely successful. However, utilizing the military for law enforcement purposes may expose the military to the same drug related corruption that is growing inside the other Mexican institutions and negatively impact the effectiveness of the military in the long term.

Mexico is faces grave threats to safety and security due to narco-violence. This same violence also threatens rule of law within Mexico. Federal judges and magistrates (particularly those attached to penal courts) are subject to daily threats culminating in a growing number of narco-related assassinations from 1987 to the present.[192] These threats can coerce favorable judgments against the powerful narco-traficantes.

The lack of safety and security even threatens the very top of the pyramid of state roles, participation and human rights. From a participation perspective, Mexico has regular elections but lots of assassinations. In addition, there is widespread intimidation prior to the elections. Armed political non-state actors are competing violently with legitimate political entities to control the government before and after elections. From a human rights perspective, the media is free from state censorship but cartels intimidate and assassinate media personalities for airing anti-cartel opinions. An example was the assassination of Paco Stanley, a popular Mexican media personality, on June 7, 1999. This marked the 630th attack against journalists just during the Zedillo presidency.[193] In addition, the use of military forces for law enforcement duties brings the risk of associated human rights violations. In conclusion, although Mexico is doing well with respect to the categories of participation and human rights, human development, and economic development, Mexico faces grave threats to safety and security and rule of law that threaten to undermine progress in the other categories of public goods and may lead to collapse. Figure 10 shows the overall performance of Mexico with regards to the delivery of public goods and highlights Mexico's weak foundation of safety and security and rule of law.

		0-25% (Poor)	25-50%	50-75%	75-100% (Good)
Participation and Human Rights	FIW				
	Polity				
	WGI				
	GGI				
	FSI				
Human Development	Polity				
	GGI				
	FSI				
Economic Development	Polity				
	FSI				
Rule of Law	FIW				
	WGI				
Safety and Security	Polity				
	WGI				
	FSI				

FIW – Freedom in the World GGI – Global Governance Initiative
Polity – Polity IV FSI – Failed States Index
WGI – Worldwide Governance Research Indicators

Figure 10: Mexico's performance in delivery of public goods.[194]

Conclusion

The threats facing Mexico uniquely illustrate that the state must structure the delivery of public goods in a sequential and hierarchical basis with safety and security and rule of law providing a foundation upon which the state builds delivery of all other public goods. Therefore, the state must pursue safety and security first, prior to exerting energy and effort into other categories. From this analysis, it is posited that a failed state is one which cannot provide the public good of safety and security. Rule of law is a concern since it provides the framework in which citizens can peacefully resolve disputes through nonviolent means. Rule of law assists the state in building the foundation of safety and security.

With the foundation of safety and security in place, the state can begin to focus on human and economic development. These categories, although important, cannot exist in an environment in which there are threats to safety and security and rule of law. As a final stage of state development, with the lower levels complete, the state can begin to deliver the public goods of participation and human rights. States must pursue their roles in a sequential and hierarchical basis with safety and security providing a firm foundation upon which to build.

These conclusions reach further than Mexico. During future military interventions in weak or failing states, the United States must first focus on ensuring that the state can provide safety and security to its citizens prior to pursuing the delivery of other public goods. American foreign policy must reflect the sequential and hierarchical basis of the role of the state. In the case of military intervention, the first priority should not be establishing a date for elections as US policy dictated in Iraq and Afghanistan. The first priority, after military intervention, must be to provide safety and security for the populace. The added implication for US policy is that autocracies are an acceptable form of government. Autocracies are a natural, organic government that grows up over time and is optimized to provide security for its citizenry. It takes time to progress up the pyramid of state roles and transition into a more representative form of government. American foreign policy must acknowledge that the growth and transition of autocracies takes time measured in hundreds of years not the short four-year election cycle of US domestic politics. Thus, the most critical task for US military leaders when conducting operations in failed or failing states is to manage the expectation of both the political leadership and the American public with regards to participation and human rights within the failed state. Although the American public and the international community believe that rapid elections are critical, safety and security must form the foundation of any stable state.

The topic of failed or failing states contains many areas suitable for future research. The first area is how to measure or quantify safety and security. This monograph identified that safety and security are the foundation which the delivery of all other public goods depends upon. Developing states need a method to measure and track their progress with regards to the safety and security of their populace in order to make appropriate policy and budgetary decisions. Another related area of future research is the appropriateness of subjective versus quantitative measures for the delivery of public goods. Many of the indices are moving from subjective measures to more quantitative measures. Each technique has strengths and weaknesses and each may be suitable for measurement of different categories of public goods. The final area of future research involves the threshold of tolerance or perception of what is acceptable. This threshold of tolerance will vary from culture to culture. Without accounting for the variances of tolerance, measurement as discussed above becomes meaningless.

Notes

1.   Todd Landman, *Issues and Methods in Comparative Politics* (New York: Routledge, 2008), 28.

2.   Noam Chomsky, *Failed States: The Abuse of Power and the Assault on Democracy* (New York: Metropolitan Books, 2006), 2.

3.   Figure created by author.

4.   Desiderius Erasmus, *The Education of a Christian Prince,* ed.. Lisa Jardine (Cambridge: Cambridge University Press, 1997), 35.

5.   Nicolo Machiavelli, *The Prince*, trans. George Bull (New York: Penguin Books, 1975), 27.

6.   Adolph Spaeth et al., trans., *Works of Martin Luther* (Philadelphia: A. J. Holman Company, 1915), 29-38.

7.   Jean Bodin, *Six Books of the Commonwealth*, trans. M. J. Tooley (Oxford: Blackwell, 1967), 40-9.

8.   R. E. Giesey et al., "Cardin le Bret and Lese Majeste," *Law and History Review* 41 (1986): 23-54.

9.   Thomas Hobbes, *Leviathan: with selected variants from the Latin edition of 1668*, ed. Edwin Curley (Indianapolis: Hackett Publishing Company, 1994), 76.

10.   Thomas Hobbes ,77.

11.   John Locke, *Two Treatises of Government* (London: C. Baldwin, 1824), 177.

12.   John Locke, 133.

13.   David Hume, *Treatise on Human Nature* (London: Longmans, 1874), 415.

14.   Charles de Secondat Montesquieu, *The Spirit of Laws* (New York: The Colonial Press, 1900), 151.

15.   Max Weber, "Politics as a Vocation," (lecture, Munich University, 1918).

16.   For expansion of the concept of realism see: George Kennan, *Memoirs: 1925-1950* (Boston: Little, Brown, 1972); Robert Jervis, *System Effects: Complexity in Political and Social Life* (Princeton: Princeton University Press, 1997); Kenneth Waltz, *Theory of International Politics* (New York: McGraw Hill, 1979); John Mearsheimer, *The Tragedy of Great Power Politics* (New York: Norton, 2001).

17.   President, Proclamation, "National Security Strategy 2006," (March 16, 2006), 3.

18.   Marina Ottoway, *Democracy Challenged: The Rise of Semi-Authoritarianism* (Washington: Carnegie Endowment for International Peace, 2003), 3.

19.   Fareed Zakaria, "The Rise of Illiberal Democracy," *Foreign Affairs*, November 1997, 11.

20.   Marie Besancon, *Good Governance Rankings: The Art of Measurement* (Cambridge, MA: World Peace Foundation, 2003), 2.

21.   An additional index, researched but not reported in this paper, is Transparency International's Corruption Perceptions Index (CPI). The CPI was created in 1994 and ranks states according to subjective measures related to corruption only. The CPI defines corruption as "the misuse of entrusted power for private gain." Many of the other indices discussed in this paper

reference the CPI to assess corruption but due to its narrow scope, this paper will not discuss it further. Transparency International, "About Transparency International," http://www.transparency. org/ about_us (accessed March 17, 2010).

22. Freedom House, "Freedom in the World 2010 Survey Release," http://www. freedomhouse.org/ template.cfm?page=505 (accessed March 17, 2010).

23. United Nations, "The Universal Declaration of Human Rights," http://www.un.org/en/ documents/udhr/ (accessed March 17, 2010).

24. Organization of the Islamic Conference, "The Cairo Declaration on Human Rights in Islam," http://www.oic-oci.org/english/article/human.htm (accessed April 20, 2010).

25. Freedom House, "Freedom in the World Methodology Summary," http://www. freedomhouse .org/uploads/fiw10/FIW_2010_Methodology_Summary.pdf (accessed March 17, 2010).

26. University of Maryland, Center for International Development and Conflict Management, Minorities at Risk Project, "Ted Robert Gurr," http://www.cidcm.umd.edu/mar/bio.asp?id=2 (accessed March 18, 2010).

27. The Center for Systemic Peace, "Polity IV Project," http://www.systemicpeace.org/ polity/polity4.htm (accessed March 18, 2010).

28. David Easton, *A Framework for Political Analysis* (Englewood Cliffs, NJ: Prentice-Hall, 1965), 184.

29. Monty Marshall and Benjamin Cole, *Global Report 2009 Conflict, Governance, and State Fragility* (Washington: Center for Systemic Peace, 2009), 2.

30. Marshall and Cole, 25.

31. World Bank, "What is meant by governance ," http://info.worldbank.org/governance/ wgi/faq.htm#1 (accessed March 18, 2010).

32. World Bank, "Governance Matters 2009," http://info.worldbank.org/governance/wgi/ (accessed March 18, 2010).

33. Daniel Kaufmann, Aart Kraay, and Massimo Mastruzzi, *Governance Matters VIII: Aggregate and Individual Governance Indicators 1996-2008* (World Bank Policy Research Working Paper no. 4978), 5.

34. World Economic Forum, "Global Governance Initiative," http://www.weforum.org/en/ initiatives/glocalgovernance/index.htm (accessed March 18, 2010).

35. United Nations, "UN Millennium Project," http://www.unmillenniumproject.org/ (accessed March 17, 2010).

36. World Economic Forum, "Global Governance Initiative," http://www.weforum.org/ en/ initiatives/glocalgovernance/index.htm (accessed March 18, 2010); United Nations, "UN Millennium Project," http://www.unmillenniumproject.org/ (accessed March 17, 2010).

37. Overseas Development Institute, "World Governance Assessment," http://www.odi.org. uk/ projects/00-07-world-governance-assessment/ (accessed March 18, 2010).

38. Overseas Development Institute, "About ODI: Our mission, people, and organization," http://www.odi.org.uk/about/default.asp (accessed March 18, 2010).

39. Goran Hyden, Julius Court, and Kenneth Mease, *Making Sense of Governance: Empirical Evidence form Sixteen Developing Countries* (Boulder, CO: Lynne Reinner Publishers, 2004), 2-3.

40. United Nations Economic Commission for Africa, *African Governance Report 2005* (Addis Ababa: ECA Documents Reproduction and Distribution Unit), xiii - xiv.

41. United Nations Economic Commission for Africa.

42. Since these two terms are grouped this implies rule of law as it relates to second generational rights not as it applies to the category rule of law. See a further discussion of these two levels of human rights in the participation and human rights section of this monograph. For more information see Karel Vasak, "Human Rights: A Thirty-Year Struggle: the Sustained Efforts to give Force of law to the Universal Declaration of Human Rights," *UNESCO Courier* 30, no. 11 (November 1977), 28-32.

43. This final category of institutional capacity building for governance did not fit within the five category framework posed within this monograph and the author categorized as miscellaneous.

44. National Bureau of Economic Research, "Index of African Governance," http://www.nber.org/ data/iag.html (accessed March 17, 2010).

45. World Peace Foundation, "Projects: Index of African Governance," http://www.worldpeacefoundation.org/africangovernance.html (accessed March 18, 2010).

46. Harvard University, John F. Kennedy School of Government, Belfer Center for Science and International Affairs, "Intrastate Conflict Program," http://belfercenter.ksg.harvard.edu/ project/52/ intrastate_conflict_program.html?page_id=223 (accessed March 18, 2010).

47. Mo Ibrahim Foundation, "The Ibrahim Index," http://www.moibrahimfoundation.org/ en/section/the-ibrahim-index (accessed March 18, 2010); African Success, "Mo Ibrahim Biographical data," http://www.africansuccess.org/ visuFiche.php?id=387&lang=en (accessed March 18, 2010). Mo Ibrahim is a wealthy Sudanese businessman. He made his fortune as a mobile communication entrepreneur.

48. Robert Rotberg, "The Failure and Collapse of Nation-States: Breakdown, Prevention, and Repair," in *When States Fail: Causes and Consequences,* ed., Robert Rotberg (Cambridge: Princeton University Press, 2003), 2-5.

49. Foreign Policy, "Failed States Index 2009," http://www.foreignpolicy.com/articles/2009/06/22/the_2009_failed_states_index (accessed March 17, 2010).

50. Pauline Baker, *The Conflict Assessment System Tool (CAST): An Analytical Model for Early Warning and Risk Assessment of Weak and Failing States* (Washington: The Fund for Peace), 9.

51. Foreign Policy, "FAQ & Methodology," http://www.foreignpolicy.com/articles/2009/06/22/2009_failed_states_index_faq_methodology (accessed March 18, 2010).

52. Foreign Policy.

53. Robert Rotberg and Rachel Gisselquist, *Index of African Governance: Results and Rankings 2008* (Cambridge, MA: Kennedy School of Government, 2009) 133.

54. Karel Vasak, "Human Rights: A Thirty-Year Struggle: the Sustained Efforts to give Force of law to the Universal Declaration of Human Rights," *UNESCO Courier* 30:11 (Paris: United

Nations Educational, Scientific, and Cultural Organization, November 1977). Human rights as defined in this monograph refer exclusively to first generation rights. Second generation rights include rights associated with equality and are social, economic, and cultural in nature.

55. Freedom House, "Freedom in the World 2010 Checklist Questions," http://www. freedomhouse. org/uploads/fiw10/FIW_2010_Checklist_Questions.pdf (accessed March 17, 2010).

56. Kaufmann, Kraay, and Mastruzzi, 6.

57. World Economic Forum, "Global Governance Initiative," http://www.weforum.org/en/ initiatives/glocalgovernance/index.htm (accessed March 17, 2010).

58. Overseas Development Institute , "Governance Assessment," http://www.odi.org.uk/ resources/ download/1321.pdf (accessed March 18, 2010).

59. United Nations Economic Commission for Africa, "African Governance Report 2005," http://www.uneca.org/agr2005/ (accessed March 18, 2010).

60. See 42.

61. Rotberg and Gisselquist, 134.

62. Fund for Peace, "Failed States Index Scores 2007," http://www.fundforpeace.org/web/ index.php?option=com_content&task=view&id=229&Itemid=366 (accessed March 18, 2010).

63. Rotberg and Gisselquist, 221.

64. Rotberg and Gisselquist, 171.

65. Fund for Peace, "Failed States Index Scores 2007," http://www.fundforpeace.org/ web/ index.php?option=com_content&task=view&id=229&Itemid=366 (accessed March 18, 2010).

66. Rotberg and Gisselquist, 97.

67. George Fletcher, *Basic Concepts of Legal Thought* (New York: Oxford University Press, 1996), 11-12. This offers the distinction between law and rights.

68. See 42.

69. Overseas Development Institute , "Governance Assessment," http://www.odi.org.uk/ resources/download/1321.pdf (accessed March 18, 2010).

70. Rotberg and Gisselquist, 45.

71. Fund for Peace, "Failed States Index Scores 2007," http://www.fundforpeace.org/ web/ index.php?option=com_content&task=view&id=229&Itemid=366 (accessed March 18, 2010).

72. Paul Collier and Nicholas Sambanis, eds., *Understanding Civil War: Evidence and Analysis, Vol. 2: Europe, Central Asia, and other regions* (Washington, DC: World Bank, 2005).

73. Paul Collier. Note: the variables of geographic dispersion of the population and size of the country are related to geography and demographics and did not fit into the author's categories of public goods.

74. The Institute for State Effectiveness, "Fixing Failed States," http://www.effectivestates. org/ (accessed March 18, 2010).

75. These groupings are the author's interpretation. The Institute for State Effectiveness only groups the responsibilities by color within the Institute for State Effectiveness logo.

76. Ashraf Ghani and Clare Lockhart, *Fixing Failed States: A Framework for Rebuilding a Fractured World* (New York: Oxford University Press, 2008).

77. The Institute for State Effectiveness, "Fixing Failed States," http://www.effectivestates. org/ (accessed March 18, 2010).

78. Abraham Maslow, *Motivation and Personality* (New York: Harper and Row, 1954), 92

79. Abraham Maslow.

80. Rotberg and Gisselquist, 8.

81. Zakaria, 1. The author attributes the quote Richard Holbrooke in reference to the 1996 elections in Bosnia.

82. James Putzel, *Overview: Crisis States Programme* (London: Crisis States Research Centre, 2003), 2.

83. Max Weber, "Politics as a Vocation," (lecture, Munich University, 1918).

84. Ralph Peters (lecture, School of Advanced Military Studies, Ft Leavenworth, KS March 10, 2010).

85. This represents the author's adaptation of Maslow's hierarchy of human needs to a hierarchy of state roles.

86. International Monetary Fund, "World Economic Outlook 2009," http://imf.org/external/ pubs/ft/weo/2009/02/ (accessed April 20, 2010).

87. Department of Energy, "World Proven Reserves of Oil and Natural Gas, 2009," http:// www.eia.doe.gov/emeu/international/reserves.html (accessed April 20, 2010).

88. Michael J. Dziedzic, *Mexico: Converging Challenges* (London: International Institute for Strategic Studies, 1989), 5.

89. Freedom House, "Analysis," http://www.freedomhouse.org/template.cfm?page=5 (accessed April 13, 2010). Download file FIW_AllScores_Countries.xls from the link "Comparative Scores". Mexico scored 2 and 3 out of 7 with 7 being the worst.

90. Marshall and Cole, 29. The Polity index scale is bounded by Somalia with a score of 25 representing poor governance.

91. World Bank, "Governance Matters 2009," http://info.worldbank.org/governance/ wgi/ sc_chart.asp (accessed April 13, 2010). The WGI does not report a composite score. The author calculated this score with a simple average of the six category scores of 50.5, 24.4, 61.1, 65.2, 29.7, and 49.8 for voice and accountability, political stability, governmental effectiveness, regulatory quality, rule of law, and control of corruption respectively. A perfect score (good governance) is 100.

92. United Nations, "MGD Monitor," http://www.mdgmonitor.org/country_progress. cfm?c= MEX&cd=484 (accessed April 13, 2010). The GGI does not report countries individually, however, the UN does track the progress of states with respect to the Millennium Challenge (MC) goals by ranking each goal as achieved, on-track, possible with changes, and off-track. Future use of the term GGI will refer to the UN MC goal scores. The author assigned each status a value with achieved = 4 and off-track = 1. The composite score is a simple average. Mexico has achieved two goals, is on-track with four goals, and goal achievement is possible for one goal.

93. Foreign Policy, "The Failed State Index 2009," http://www.foreignpolicy.com/articles/ 2009/06/22/2009_failed_states_index_interactive_map_and_rankings (accessed April 13, 2010). Mexico scored 75.4 out of 120 with 120 representing poor governance.

94. The author adapted each ranking system to a percentage score with 100% representing good delivery of public goods and 0% representing poor delivery of public goods. Freedom House score is a simple average of the two categories scores converted to a percentage. Mexico scored 2 for political rights and 3 for civil liberties on a seven point scale where 7 represents poor governance. This result is inverted to make higher scores representative of good governance. Polity IV score is normalized to 100 by using Somalia's score of 25 to represent poor governance and inverted to ensure higher numbers represent good governance. The WGI score is a simple average of the six categories rated by the WGI (it is already on a 100 point scale with higher scores representing good governance). The GGI score is a simple average of the seven categories rated by the GGI (neglecting the global partnership). This average is normalized to a percentage score. The Failed States Index is normalized utilizing a score of 120 and inverted to ensure that higher scores represent good governance.

95. Freedom House, "Analysis."

96. Marshall and Cole, pg 29.

97. World Bank, "Governance Matters 2009."

98. Method used to normalize data is identical to that used in Table 4. Polity IV utilizes color assessment for its subcategories that were not utilized in the overall ranking. The author assigned values to each color, then used a simple average normalized to a percentage scale and inverted to account for multiple Polity IV assessments within one category of public good. Black / extremely fragile = 4, Red / highly fragile = 3, Orange / moderately fragile = 2, yellow / low fragility = 1, and green / no fragility = 0. The Failed State Index subcategory scores were grouped with a simple average and normalized to 10 and inverted so that higher scores represent good delivery of public goods.

99. United Nations, "MGD Monitor."

100. Foreign Policy, "Failed States Index 2009."

101. Donald Schulz, *Mexico in Crisis* (Carlisle Barracks, PA: US Army War College, 1995), 1. The author attributed the quotation to Mario Vargas Llosa.

102. Judith Hellman, *Mexico in Crisis* (New York: Holmes & Meier, 1978), 100.

103. Dziedzic, 48.

104. Dziedzic, 28.

105. Dziedzic, 29.

106. Robert Kossick, "The Rule of Law and Development in Mexico," *Arizona Journal of International and Comparative Law* 21, no. 3 (2004): 715-834.

107. Robert Dahl, *Polyarchy: Participation and Opposition* (New Haven: Yale University Press 1971), 13.

108. Alejandro Munoz, "Transnational and Domestic Processes in the Definition of Human Rights Policies in Mexico," *Human Rights Quarterly* 31, no. 1 (February 2009): 36.

109. Hugo Alejandro Concha Cantu, "The Justice System: Judiciary, Military, and Human Rights," in *Changing Structure of Mexico: Political, Social, and Economic Prospects*, ed. Laura Randal (New York: M. E. Sharpe, 2006) 261, 378-80.

110. Human Rights Watch (HRW), *Justice in Jeopardy: Why Mexico's First Real Effort to Address Past Abuses Risks Becoming its Latest Failure* (New York: Human Rights Watch, 2003), 4-6.

111. HRW, *The New Year's Rebellion: Violation of Human Rights and Humanitarian Law During the Armed Revolt in Chiapas, Mexico* (New York: Human Rights Watch, 1994), 7-9.

112. UN Commission on Human Rights, 57th Session, statement submitted by Jorge Castaneda, Minister for Foreign Affairs of Mexico, 2001.

113. Margaret Keck and Kathryn Sikkink, *Activist Beyond Borders: Advocacy Networks in International Politics* (Ithaca, NY: Cornell University Press, 1998) 110-115.

114. HRW, Justice in Jeopardy, 7-8.

115. Kossick, 816.

116. Marshall and Cole, 29.

117. United Nations, "MGD Monitor."

118. Foreign Policy, "Failed States Index 2009."

119. Method used to normalize data is identical to that used in previous tables.

120. Dziedzic, 24.

121. Lucrecia Santibanez, Georges Vernez, and Paula Razquin, *Education in Mexico: Challenges and Opportunities* (Santa Monica, CA: RAND Corporation, 2005), 65.

122. Lucrecia Santibanez, Georges Vernez, and Paula Razquin, 16.

123. Lucrecia Santibanez, Georges Vernez, and Paula Razquin, 12.

124. Lucrecia Santibanez, Georges Vernez, and Paula Razquin, 69-70.

125. Lucrecia Santibanez, Georges Vernez, and Paula Razquin, vii.

126. Marshall and Cole, 29.

127. Foreign Policy, "Failed States Index 2009."

128. Method used to normalize data is identical to that used in previous tables

129. Dziedzic, 12.

130. Dziedzic, 10.

131. Associated Press, "Mexico Inflation Down," *New York Times*, January 11, 1989.

132. Amnesty International, "Amnesty International Report: 1987," (London: Amnesty International, 1987), 185-6.

133. Alan Riding, *Mexico: Inside the Volcano* (London: I.B. Tauris, 1987), 98.

134. During the Echeverria era, the government moved beyond regulation into ownership of a broad range of enterprises. These government owned companies were called *parastatals*.

135. A factory which imports materials and equipment on a duty-free and tariff-free basis for assembly or manufacturing and then re-exports the assembled product, usually back to the originating country is referred to as a *maquiladora*.

136. North American Free Trade Agreement Implementation Act, Pub. L. No. 103-182, 107 Stat. 2057, USC. 3311.

137. Ranko Oliver, "In the Twelve Years of NAFTA, the Treaty Gave to Me ... What, Exactly?: An Assessment of Economic, Social, and Political Developments in Mexico Since 1994 and Their Impact on Mexican Immigration into the United States," *Harvard Latino Law Review* 10 (Spring 2007), 58.

138. US Department of State, "NAFTA Partners Celebrate Tenth Anniversary of Trade Agreement (Oct. 8, 2003)," http://www.america.gov/st/washfile-english/2003/October/20031008164448 rellims0.4990198.html (accessed April 20, 2010.)

139. Global Britain, "European Union 2003 Prosperity Rankings," http://www.globalbritain.org/BNN/BN35.pdf (accessed April 20, 2010).

140. Mark Weisbrot, David Rosnik, and Dean Baker., *Getting Mexico to Grow with NAFTA: The World Bank's Analysis* (Washington: Center for Economic and Policy Research, 2004).

141. Oliver, 80.

142. Office of the US Trade Representative, "NAFTA at 10: Myth - NAFTA was a Failure for Mexico," http://www.ustr.gov/about-us/press-office/fact-sheets/archives/2003/november/nafta-10-myth-nafta-was-failure-mexico (accessed April 20, 2010).

143. Oliver, 72.

144. Daniel Lederman, William Maloney, and Luis Serven, Lessons from NAFTA for Latin America & the Caribbean Countries: A Summary of Research Findings (Washington: World Bank, 2003).

145. Stephen Johnson, *Is Neoliberalism Dead in Latin America?* (Washington: The Heritage Foundation, 2003).

146. Mary Jordan, "The Bribes that Bind Mexico – and Hold It Back," *Washington Post*, April 18, 2004.

147. Kossick, 723. The author attributes the quotation to Alejandro Ascencio.

148. Method used to normalize data is identical to that used in previous tables.

149. Freedom House, "Analysis."

150. World Bank, "Governance Matters 2009."

151. Bonnie Palifka, "Trade Liberalization and Bribes," http://homepages.mty.itesm.mx/bpalifka/customs.pdf (accessed April 20, 2010).

152. Carlos Vazquez, trans., *The Political Constitution of the Mexican United States*, (Mexico City: Universidad Nacional Autonoma de Mexico, 2005).

153. David Luhnow, "Presumption of Guilt," *Wall Street Journal*, October 17, 2009. In 2008, the Mexican Congress amended their Constitution to incorporate the presumption of innocence into modern Mexican law, as well as allow oral trials in most cases. However, Mexican states will have until 2016 to implement the changes.

154. David Luhnow.

155. Alberto Szekely, "Democracy, Judicial Reform, the Rule of Law, and Environmental Justice in Mexico," *Houston Journal of International Law* 21, no. 3 (1999), 385-388.

156. James Mahon, "Reforms in the Administration of Justice in Latin America: Overview and Emerging Trends" in *Reinventing Leviathan,* ed. Ben Schneider (Miami: University of Miami Iberian Studies Institute, 2003), 251-254.

157. US Department of State, "Mexico," *Country Reports on Human Rights Practices for 1994* (Washington: US Government Printing Office, February 1995), 447.

158. Kossick, 750.

159. Kossick, 751.

160. Kossick, 754.

161. Luhnow. The author attributes this data to Guillermo Zepeda, a CIDE scholar. .

162. Luhnow. The author attributes this data to a survey of 400 criminal cases in Mexico City carried out by National Center for State Courts, a US nonprofit organization.

163. Victor Fuentes, "Rebasan denuncias al sistema judicial," *Reforma*, June 24, 2002.

164. Luhnow.

165. Kossick, 791.

166. Kossick, 814. Includes data for number of days to enforce a contract and evict a tenant. As well as poll data for questions regarding a fair and impartial court system, a honest and uncorrupt court system, a court system able to enforce decisions, quality of justice, and confidence in the Mexican supreme court. All the indicators for Mexico are poor.

167. Kossick, 718.

168. Alicia Yamin and Pilar Garcia, "The Absence of the Rule of Law in Mexico: Diagnosis and Implications for a Mexican Transition to Democracy," *Loyola of LA International and Comparative Law Journal* 21 (July 1999): 467-520.

169. Kossick, 811.

170. Hernando de Soto, *The Mystery of Capital* (New York: Basic Books, 2000), 154-159.

171. Hobbes, 84.

172. Marshall and Cole, 29.

173. World Bank, "Governance Matters 2009.".

174. United Nations, "MDG Monitor."

175. Foreign Policy, "Failed States Index 2009."

176. Method used to normalize data is identical to that used in previous tables

177. US Department of State, "Travel Warning," http://travel.state.gov/travel/ cis_pa_tw/tw/ tw 4755.html, (accessed 19 March 2010).

178. Barnard Thompson, "Kidnapping are out of Control in Mexico," http://mexidata.info/ id217.html (accessed April 20, 2010).

179. Jordan, The Bribes that Bind Mexico – and Hold It Back.

180. Richard B. Craig, "Mexican Narcotics Traffic: Bi-national Security Implications," in *The Latin American Narcotics Trade and US National Security,* ed. Donald Mabry (Westport, CT: Greenwood, 1989), 28-30, 33-34.

181. Daniel Kurtz-Phelan, "The Long War of Genaro García Luna," *New York Times*, July 13, 2008.

182. Becky Branford, "Mexico fights spectre of narcopolitics," *BBC News*, February 22, 2005.

183. CNN, "Mexico drug fighter killed after less than a day on job (February 4, 2009),"
http://www.cnn.com/2009/WORLD/americas/02/04/mexico.general/index.html, (accessed 13
April 2010).

184. CNN.

185. David Luhnow and Jose de Cordoba, "The Perilous State of Mexico," Wall Street
Journal, February 21, 2009.

186. Hal Brands, *Mexico's Narco-insurgency and US Counterdrug Policy*, (Carlisle, PA: US
Army War College, 2009), 8.

187. Kurtz-Phelan.

188. Sam Logan, "The Evolution of 'Los Zetas,' a Mexican Crime Organization," http://
mexidata.info/id2194.html, (accessed 19 March 2010).

189. Brands, 11.

190. Luhnow and Cordoba.

191. Alfredo Corchado and Irene Barcenas, "Mexico denies high numbers of deserters,"
Dallas Morning News, January 5, 2006.

192. Kevin Sullivan, "Mexican Judges' Climate of Fear," *Washington Post*, November 19,
2001.

193. Al Giordano, "Narco-media: Drug Corruption in the Press from Mexico to the US,"
http://www.mediachannel.org/originals/narcomedia.shtml (accessed April 20, 2010).

194.   This figure is based on the author's analysis of the ranking systems in the preceding
sections normalizing the indices to a percentile scale with higher scores representing good
governance and delivery of public goods.

Bibliography

African Success. "Mo Ibrahim Biographical data." http://www.africansuccess.org/ visuFiche.php?id=387&lang=en (accessed March 18, 2010).

Bodin, Jean. *Six Books of the Commonwealth*. Translated by M. J. Tooley. Oxford: Blackwell, 1967.

Cantu, Hugo Alejandro Concha. "The Justice System: Judiciary, Military, and Human Rights." In *Changing Structure of Mexico: Political, Social, and Economic Prospects*. Edited by Laura Randal. New York: M. E. Sharpe, 2006.

Center for Systemic Peace. "Polity IV Project." http://www.systemicpeace.org/ polity/polity4.htm (accessed March 18, 2010).

Chomsky, Noam. *Failed States: The Abuse of Power and the Assault on Democracy*. New York: Metropolitan Books, 2006.

Collier, Paul and Nicholas Sambanis, eds. *Understanding Civil War: Evidence and Analysis, Vol. 2: Europe, Central Asia, and other regions*. Washington, DC: World Bank, 2005.

Craig, Richard B. "Mexican Narcotics Traffic: Bi-national Security Implications." In *The Latin American Narcotics Trade and US National Security*. Edited by Donald Mabry. Westport, CT: Greenwood, 1989.

Dahl, Robert. *Polyarchy: Participation and Opposition*. New Haven: Yale University Press 1971.

de Soto, Hernando. *The Mystery of Capital*. New York: Basic Books, 2000.

Easton, David. *A Framework for Political Analysis*. Englewood Cliffs, NJ: Prentice-Hall, 1965.

Erasmus, Desiderius. *The Education of a Christian Prince*. Edited by Lisa Jardine. Cambridge: Cambridge University Press, 1997.

Fletcher, George. *Basic Concepts of Legal Thought*. New York: Oxford University Press, 1996.

Foreign Policy. "The Failed State Index 2009." http://www.foreignpolicy.com/ articles/ 2009/06/22/2009_failed_states_index_interactive_map_and_rankings (accessed April 13, 2010).

Foreign Policy. "FAQ & Methodology." http://www.foreignpolicy.com/articles/ 2009/06/22/2009_failed_states_index_faq_methodology (accessed March 18, 2010).

Freedom House. "Analysis." http://www.freedomhouse.org/template.cfm?page=5 (accessed April 13, 2010).

Freedom House. "Freedom in the World 2010 Checklist Questions." http://www. freedomhouse. org/uploads/fiw10/FIW_2010_Checklist_Questions.pdf (accessed March 17, 2010).

Freedom House. "Freedom in the World 2010 Survey Release." http://www. freedomhouse.org/ template.cfm?page=505 (accessed March 17, 2010).

Freedom House. "Freedom in the World Methodology Summary." http://www. freedomhouse .org/uploads/fiw10/FIW_2010_Methodology_Summary.pdf (accessed March 17, 2010).

Fund for Peace. "Failed States Index Scores 2007." http://www.fundforpeace.org/ web/ index.php?option=com_content&task=view&id=229&Itemid=366 (accessed March 18, 2010).

Ghani, Ashraf and Clare Lockhart. *Fixing Failed States: A Framework for Rebuilding a Fractured World.* New York: Oxford University Press, 2008.

Giesey, R. E., Lanny Haldy, and James Millhorn. "Cardin le Bret and Lese Majeste." *Law and History Review* 4, no. 1 (Spring 1986): 23-54.

Giordano, Al. "Narco-media: Drug Corruption in the Press from Mexico to the US." http://www.mediachannel.org/originals/narcomedia.shtml (accessed April 20, 2010).

Global Britain. "European Union 2003 Prosperity Rankings." http://www. globalbritain.org/BNN/BN35.pdf (accessed April 20, 2010).

Belfer Center for Science and International Affairs. "Intrastate Conflict Program." Harvard University. http://belfercenter.ksg.harvard.edu/project/52/ intrastate_conflict_program.html?page_id=223 (accessed March 18, 2010).

Hellman, Judith. *Mexico in Crisis.* New York: Holmes & Meier, 1978.

Hobbes, Thomas. *Leviathan: with selected variants from the Latin edition of 1668.* Edited by Edwin Curley. Indianapolis: Hackett Publishing Company, 1994.

Hume, David. *Treatise on Human Nature.* London: Longmans, 1874.

Institute for State Effectiveness. "Fixing Failed States." http://www.effectivestates. org/ (accessed March 18, 2010).

International Monetary Fund. "World Economic Outlook 2009." http://imf.org/ external/ pubs/ft/weo/2009/02/ (accessed April 20, 2010).

Jervis, Robert. *System Effects: Complexity in Political and Social Life.* Princeton: Princeton University Press, 1997.

Keck, Margaret and Kathryn Sikkink. *Activist Beyond Borders: Advocacy Networks in International Politics.* Ithaca, NY: Cornell University Press, 1998.

Kennan, George. *Memoirs: 1925-1950.* Boston: Little, Brown, 1972.

Kossick, Robert. "The Rule of Law and Development in Mexico." *Arizona Journal of International and Comparative Law* 21, no. 3 (2004): 715-834.

Landman, Todd. *Issues and Methods in Comparative Politics.* New York: Routledge, 2008.

Locke, John. *Two Treatises of Government.* London: C. Baldwin, 1824.

Logan, Sam. "The Evolution of 'Los Zetas,' a Mexican Crime Organization." Mexidata. http://mexidata.info/id2194.html. (accessed 19 March 2010).

Luther, Martin. *Works of Martin Luther.* Edited and translated by Adolph Spaeth, L.D. Reed, and Henry Eyster Jacobs. Philadelphia: A. J. Holman Company, 1915.

Machiavelli, Nicolo. *The Prince.* Translated by George Bull. New York: Penguin Books, 1975.

Mahon, James. "Reforms in the Administration of Justice in Latin America: Overview and Emerging Trends." In *Reinventing Leviathan*, edited by Ben Schneider. Miami: University of Miami Iberian Studies Institute, 2003.

Maslow, Abraham. *Motivation and Personality.* New York: Harper and Row, 1954.

Mearsheimer, John. *The Tragedy of Great Power Politics.* New York: Norton, 2001.

Mo Ibrahim Foundation. "The Ibrahim Index." http://www.moibrahimfoundation.org/en/section/the-ibrahim-index (accessed March 18, 2010).

Montesquieu, Charles de Secondat. *The Spirit of Laws.* New York: The Colonial Press, 1900.

Munoz, Alejandro. "Transnational and Domestic Processes in the Definition of Human Rights Policies in Mexico." *Human Rights Quarterly* 31, no. 1 (February 2009): 35-58.

National Bureau of Economic Research. "Index of African Governance." http://www.nber.org/ data/iag.html (accessed March 17, 2010).

Office of the US Trade Representative. "NAFTA at 10: Myth - NAFTA was a Failure for Mexico." http://www.ustr.gov/about-us/press-office/fact-sheets/archives/2003/november/nafta-10-myth-nafta-was-failure-mexico (accessed April 20, 2010).

Oliver, Ranko. "In the Twelve Years of NAFTA, the Treaty Gave to Me … What, Exactly?: An Assessment of Economic, Social, and Political Developments in Mexico Since 1994 and Their Impact on Mexican Immigration into the United States." *Harvard Latino Law Review* 10 (Spring 2007): 53-134.

Organization of the Islamic Conference. "The Cairo Declaration on Human Rights in Islam." http://www.oic-oci.org/english/article/human.htm (accessed April 20, 2010).

Ottoway, Marina. *Democracy Challenged: The Rise of Semi-Authoritarianism.* Washington: Carnegie Endowment for International Peace, 2003.

Overseas Development Institute. "About ODI: Our mission, people, and organization." http://www.odi.org.uk/about/default.asp (accessed March 18, 2010).

Overseas Development Institute. "Governance Assessment." http://www.odi.org.uk/resources/ download/1321.pdf (accessed March 18, 2010).

Overseas Development Institute. "World Governance Assessment." http://www.odi.org.uk/ projects/00-07-world-governance-assessment/ (accessed March 18, 2010).

Palifka, Bonnie. "Trade Liberalization and Bribes." http://homepages.mty.itesm.mx/bpalifka/customs.pdf (accessed April 20, 2010).

Peters, Ralph. Lecture, School of Advanced Military Studies, Ft Leavenworth, KS, March 10, 2010.

Riding, Alan. *Mexico: Inside the Volcano*. London: I.B. Tauris, 1987.

Rotberg, Robert. "The Failure and Collapse of Nation-States: Breakdown, Prevention, and Repair." In *When States Fail: Causes and Consequences*. Edited by Robert Rotberg. Cambridge: Princeton University Press, 2003.

Szekely, Alberto. "Democracy, Judicial Reform, the Rule of Law, and Environmental Justice in Mexico." *Houston Journal of International Law* 21, no.3 (1999): 385-424.

Thompson, Barnard. "Kidnappings are out of Control in Mexico." http://mexidata.info/ id217.html (accessed April 20, 2010).

Transparency International. "About Transparency International." http://www.transparency.org/ about_us (accessed March 17, 2010).

United Nations. "The Universal Declaration of Human Rights." http://www.un.org/en/ documents/udhr/ (accessed March 17, 2010).

United Nations. "MGD Monitor." http://www.mdgmonitor.org/country_progress.cfm?c= MEX&cd=484 (accessed April 13, 2010).

United Nations. "UN Millennium Project." http://www.unmillenniumproject.org/ (accessed March 17, 2010).

United Nations Economic Commission for Africa. "African Governance Report 2005." http://www.uneca.org/agr2005/ (accessed March 18, 2010).

US Department of Energy. "World Proven Reserves of Oil and Natural Gas, 2009." http://www.eia.doe.gov/emeu/international/reserves.html (accessed April 20, 2010).

US Department of State. "NAFTA Partners Celebrate Tenth Anniversary of Trade Agreement (Oct. 8, 2003)." http://www.america.gov/st/washfile-english/2003/October/20031008164448 rellims0.4990198.html (accessed April 20, 2010.)

US Department of State. "Travel Warning." http://travel.state.gov/travel/ cis_pa_tw/tw/tw_4755.html, (accessed 19 March 2010).

US President, Proclamation. "National Security Strategy 2006." (March 16, 2006).

Minorities at Risk Project. "Ted Robert Gurr." University of Maryland. http://www.cidcm.umd.edu/mar/bio.asp?id=2 (accessed March 18, 2010).

Vasak, Karel. "Human Rights: A Thirty-Year Struggle: the Sustained Efforts to give Force of Law to the Universal Declaration of Human Rights." *UNESCO Courier* 30, no. 11 (1977): 28-32.

Vazquez, Carlos, trans. *The Political Constitution of the Mexican United States*. Mexico City: Universidad Nacional Autonoma de Mexico, 2005.

Waltz, Kenneth. *Theory of International Politics*. New York: McGraw Hill, 1979.

Weber, Max. "Politics as a Vocation." Lecture, Munich University, 1918.

World Bank. "Governance Matters 2009." http://info.worldbank.org/governance/wgi/ sc_chart.asp (accessed April 13, 2010).

World Bank. "What is meant by governance." http://info.worldbank.org/governance/ wgi/faq.htm#1 (accessed March 18, 2010).

World Economic Forum. "Global Governance Initiative." http://www.weforum.org/ en/ initiatives/glocalgovernance/index.htm (accessed March 18, 2010).

World Peace Foundation. "Projects: Index of African Governance." http://www. worldpeacefoundation.org/africangovernance.html (accessed March 18, 2010).

Yamin, Alicia and Pilar Garcia. "The Absence of the Rule of Law in Mexico: Diagnosis and Implications for a Mexican Transition to Democracy." *Loyola of LA International and Comparative Law Journal* 21 (July 1999): 467-520.

Toward Development of Afghanistan National Stability: Analyses in Historical, Military, and Cultural Contexts

Lieutenant Colonel Christopher D. Dessaso

American policy in Afghanistan has evolved since the initial engagement of US forces in Afghanistan in 2002. It has become increasingly clear the strategic focus must include a plan to concentrate upon and continue the development of a stable and secure central government supported appropriately by an Afghan National Military. The evolution and progression of the central government as well as the Afghan National Army has become an essential task in the Afghanistan War.

This monograph researches the history of some of Afghanistan's key governing regimes with a focus primarily upon governance, military, economic, and social factors of these previous governments and the national militaries which underpinned these regimes beginning in the mid-nineteenth century through the end of the twentieth century. The intention of this research is to identify potential operational level lessons learned that may assist coalition planners in developing the current and future Afghan National Army toward ensuring a stable and successful central government in Afghanistan. The research further includes discussion and analyses of the culture and geography of Afghanistan as essential factors to be considered. These research findings will provide coalition planners additional means to discover and evaluate possible solutions to the fundamental task of establishing an effective Afghan military which is essential to the creation of a successful, legitimate, and stable central government.

Historical overview of eight national military regimes from 1860 to 1992 and a more detailed analysis of successes and failures of three of these regimes will provide insight and assistance toward the development of the central government and Afghan National Military for the near and further terms. This historical discussion will be examined with respect to the role of a central Afghanistan government and the level of control it may exert upon a national military, cultural factors, geography, and influence of foreign governments. Further analysis within the context of Operation Enduring Freedom and the International Security Assistance Force will provide insight and conclusions of use to coalition planners.

Introduction

In 2009 the United States Defense Department assessed the security situation in Afghanistan as deteriorating. President Barack Obama announced sweeping changes in both his 27 March and 1 December speeches in which he outlined the details of new strategy. On 27 March 2009, President Obama restated the mission of United States Forces in Afghanistan. The development of the Afghanistan National Army had become an essential task in the Afghanistan War. In the speech that outlined his new policy he addressed the Afghanistan Security Forces. The new strategy he outlined will increase the total number of the Afghan National Army (ANA) from 90,000 to 134,000 and accelerate the timeline from 2014 to 2011.[1]

This policy reversed the American policy under President George W. Bush in which the size of the Afghan Security Forces was limited due to long term cost implications.[2]

Since President Obama's 27 March speech, the discussion concerning Afghanistan has emerged to one concerning American strategy, troop strength, and the corruption of the recent Afghan elections.

Among the administration's initial changes were a 21,000 troop increase in February and a change in the NATO and International Security Assistance Force (ISAF) leadership as General Stanley McChrystal was appointed as the new commander, replacing General David McKiernan in May.[3] General McChrystal conducted a thorough analysis and review of the entire ISAF mission in Afghanistan.[4] The assessment had four main points: (1) Change strategy to focus on protecting the population rather than killing the insurgents; (2) there were twelve to eighteen months to act or there could be mission failure; (3) Afghan security forces should be increased beyond the (then) goal of 220,000 to 400,000 (240,000 ANA and 160,000 Afghan National Police [ANP]); and (4) the need to increase troop levels in order to successfully implement the new strategy.

General McChrystal submitted his review along with a request for additional forces to President Obama in August. In December, President Obama issued updated guidance and US strategy for Afghanistan that included an additional troop increase of 30,000 US forces.[5] The US troop increase was followed by an additional 9,000 troops promised from the coalition allies.[6] The focus and scope of the war had been changed in order to provide time and space for the Afghanistan government to build the needed capacity to succeed.

This monograph researches the history of the Afghanistan National Military beginning in the mid-nineteenth century through the end of the twentieth century in order to identify possible operational level lessons learned that may assist coalition planners developing the current Afghanistan National Army. The research includes consideration of the culture and geography of Afghanistan as essential factors to be considered. The findings may provide future coalition planners and researchers additional means to identify or evaluate possible solutions to the essential task of developing an effective national military and establishing a stable effective central government in Afghanistan in support of United States and NATO objectives.

From 1863 through 2001 Afghanistan developed eight distinct regimes that had a nationally based military system. The historical analysis of these regimes and the successes and failures they experienced provide possible operational lessons learned that could assist in the current effort to develop the present Afghan National Military. This monograph will provide an overview of Afghanistan's history beginning with the regime of Amir Sher Ali Khan (1863-1878), followed by the regimes of Amir Abdur Rahman Khan (1880-1901), Habibullah (1901-1919), King Amanullah (1919-1929), Nadir Shah (1929-1933), King Zaher (1933-1973), Soviet Communist influence, and finally ending with the post-communist regime (1992-2001).[7] A detailed analysis will focus on three of the regimes; Abdur Rahman Khan, King Amanullah, and Nadir Shah, in order to compare and contrast them with the current operations being conducted by NATO and ISAF forces. This monograph will identify findings and suggest possible areas of potential use for future planners or researchers.

Afghanistan rebuilt its national military three times following civil war or foreign invasions.[8] Throughout its history, tribal support and popular uprisings were utilized to defend against foreign invaders and suppress domestic rebellions. The historically weak past Afghan central governments obtained varying degrees of control utilizing a variety of methods in attempting to rule.[9] Analysis of the history of Afghanistan reveals that when the nation was ruled by a strong national leader (executive), supported by the tribal chiefs and religious leaders, and backed by a strong centrally controlled professional national military, there has been internal stability. Also, when the government has attempted to implement radical social or economic reform or modernization without consolidating military control and strengthening the central government, disaster has followed. Further historical analysis reveals the impact on Afghanistan due to the interference of foreign countries, particularly Russia and Great Britain.

The analysis of the period of Afghanistan's history explored in this monograph identifies four key factors for consideration that may reveal findings that could be used to suggest potential areas to exploit in order to develop a national military capable of supporting the Afghan government. These factors are: (1) Afghanistan has produced a national military controlled by a centralized government in the past, (2) cultural, religious, and ethnic factors have played a key role in Afghanistan contributing to the success or failure of past Afghan central governments and national militaries, (3) the geography of Afghanistan is a key factor to the development and stability of a central government and utilization of the national military, and (4) the assistance or interference of foreign governments has been a key factor to the success or failure of past Afghanistan governments.

The analysis of these factors will provide the context of possible operational lessons learned for coalition planners developing the Afghanistan Security Forces. The remainder of this monograph will analyze each of these factors, beginning with the geography and demographics, and then the history and culture of Afghanistan from the mid-nineteenth century through the current situation.

Afghanistan Overview

Afghanistan is 652,230 square kilometers, the 48th largest country in the world, slightly smaller than the state of Texas.[10] The climate is arid to semiarid with hot summers and cold winters. The terrain is mostly mountainous, dominated by the Hindu Kush, with plains in the north and southwest. Afghanistan is bordered in the west with a 936 kilometer border with Iran, in the northwest by a 744 kilometer border with Turkmenistan, to the north by a 137 kilometer border with Uzbekistan, in the northeast by a 1,206 kilometer border with Tajikistan, further east by a slight 76 kilometer border with China, and to the south by the highly contentious 2,430 kilometer border with Pakistan.[11] There is one major road system that runs the outer circumference of Afghanistan through most of the major cities, as well as a highway from Kabul through the Khyber Pass into Pakistan.[12] The road network serves as the major line of communication in the country and requires security to protect the flow of supplies, equipment and travel. The road from Kabul to Peshawar is a "strategic route that carries 75% of supplies used by US and NATO forces."[13]

Afghanistan's geographical terrain physically divided the country into the major cities such as Kabul and Kandahar versus the rural areas which are populated with small villages and tribal communities. The harsh physical terrain challenged the central governments in the major cities from providing services to the rural communities where the majority of Afghans live. Afghanistan's geographical location made it a point of intersection between the Russian/Soviet regimes and the British Empire for three hundred years. Afghanistan has had constant conflict along its external borders as well as constant foreign interference and intervention which resulted in four wars and internal instability.[14] The situation was permanently aggravated due to the illogical setting up of Afghanistan's external borders, particularly the 1893 Durand line, which split the posturing tribes along the southern Afghan and northwest Pakistan borders, creating conflict in the Federal Autonomous Tribal Areas (FATA).[15]

The population is estimated at more than 28 million, with 53% of the population between the ages of fifteen and sixty-four, and a median age of seventeen. Less than two and one half percent of the population is older than sixty-four years old.[16] Population is 80% Sunni Muslim and 19% Shia. Ethnically there are 42% Pashtun, 27% Tajik, 9% Hazara, 9% Uzbek, 3% Turkmen, 2% Baloch, and 4% other. Approximately twenty-four percent of the population lives in urban centers. Demographically the Pashtuns reside mainly in the southern and eastern regions, although there are small numbers in the major cities in the north and west. The Tajiks dominate the northeastern region along the Tajikistan border and also heavily populate the major cities throughout Afghanistan except for Khandahar and Farah which are dominated by the Pashtuns. The Hazaras reside in the mountainous center of the country while the Uzbeks consolidate in the north, centered on Mazar-e-Sharif. The Turkmen straddle the length of the Turkmenistan border and the Balochs straddle the Pakistan border across from Baluchistan. There is also a small Nuristan enclave northeast of Kabul.[17]

Afghanistan's first ruler was Ahmad Shah Abdali (Durrani), a heroic twenty-five year old Afghan cavalry leader, who was selected at a "Loya Jirga" (council of nobles) in Kandahar in 1747 and remained in power until his death in 1772.[18] Ahmad Shah consolidated and enlarged Afghanistan. He defeated the Moguls west of the Indus, and he took Herat away from the Persians. Ahmad Shah Durrani's empire extended from Central Asia to Delhi, from Kashmir to the Arabian Sea.[19] Afghanistan was the greatest Muslim empire in the second half of the 18th century. Ahmad Shah, the greatest of all Afghan rulers, died of cancer at age 50.[20]

Dost Mohammad Khan, was ruler from 1826 until his death in 1863, except for the period of the First Afghan War, 1839-1842. He came to power after a civil war caused by a power struggle and years of internal fighting and chaos.[21] During his first ten year period, he spent fighting the Persians and consolidating the Afghans with mixed results. He was gaining momentum towards reunifying all of Afghanistan when Great Britain invaded and started the First Afghan War.[22]

In 1868 Sher Ali gained power and ruled until his death in 1879 at Mazar-e-Sharif during the Second Afghan War (1878-1880). Sher Ali constructed the first modern Afghan

National Army that included a system of recruitment, considerations of ethnic balancing, as well as integration of irregular troops in order to free the government of their dependence upon tribal forces.[23] Sher Ali's rule bore the brunt of the "Great Game."[24] The "Great Game" was the name given to the international policies pursued by the British Empire and the Russian Empire/Soviet Union involving Afghanistan throughout the eighteenth, nineteenth, and twentieth centuries. Afghanistan became the strategic "buffer zone" used by both Great Britain and Russia.[25]

Afghanistan has reconstructed the national military three times in the aftermath of civil war or foreign invasions, each case subjective to the "prevailing political and social conditions."[26] Historically, the Afghan state relied upon tribal support and popular uprisings to repel foreign invaders and quash domestic rebellions with a traditionally weak central government exerting varying degrees of control.[27] A detailed analysis of the history of Afghanistan reveals that when Afghanistan had a strong legitimately selected leader, supported by the trial chiefs and backed by a strong centrally controlled military, there was internal stability that allowed the ruler to govern.

Section I: Abdur Rahman Khan

Abdur Rahman Khan (1880-1901), known as the "Iron Amir," established the structure and framework for the modern state of Afghanistan and developed a grand strategy based in nationalism and Islam that would be considered by all of the future leaders of Afghanistan for years to come.[28] Through military, political, and social coercion he brought internal stability to Afghanistan. In foreign affairs, he was trapped between the Russian and British empires' expansionist policies which eventually established the current national borders of Afghanistan. Although he received financial support from Great Britain, he had no influence over his country's foreign policy. His positive legacy was Afghan nationalism over religious or tribal considerations. His negative legacy was the brutality it took to stabilize his country and the fact that he was a pawn in the British and Russian establishment of Afghanistan's international borders, especially the Durand line that splits the Pashtun tribal areas between the southern Afghan borders with Pakistan.[29]

Governance

Abdur Rahman established an Islamic based monarchy/dictatorship and developed three principles for governing Afghanistan: government control over the tribes, consolidating power through the military, and reinforcing the power of the ruler. To these ends he established a strong executive branch supported by a centrally controlled, powerful military and a supreme council (cabinet), a judiciary based upon Shari'a law but controlled by the King not the mullahs, a General Assembly (Loya Jirga) that included elites, tribal leaders, and religious leaders that could advise but not legislate.[30] Abdur Rahman believed in Afghan nationalism based in Islam. The king established himself as the religious leader of the country, as well as the political and judicial decision maker.[31] Abdur Rahman exercised "internal imperialism" that employed the military, regional administrators, and a national spy network that allowed him to consolidate his power and stabilize the country.[32] Through his spy network he was able to identify agitators, many of whom were jailed, exiled, or executed. The military dealt harshly with tribes that caused trouble. This included relocation and even conversion to Islam. To maintain order, he established provinces apart from the tribal footprint and appointed regional governors.[33] He also implemented a civil administration system that survived nearly eighty years. All of this allowed him to supersede the tribal influences and penetrate the rural areas of Afghanistan.

In international relations he understood that Afghanistan was the buffer state between Russian (on northern and western borders) and Great Britain (on southern and eastern borders). Great Britain subsidized him (from 1.2 million to 1.85 million Indian rupees per year during his regime), but he did not provoke the Russians and sought to maintain balanced relationships between the two countries.[34] The Treaty of Gandamak made Afghanistan a pseudo colony of Great Britain and took away Afghanistan's right to conduct its own international affairs. Britain originally imposed the treaty upon the previous regime and forced Abdur Rahman to adhere to the mandate as well. Over the course of his rule, the Russians and Britain continued to adjust the borders of Afghanistan in their own interests. In 1893, the British commissioned Sir Mortimer Durand to designate the boundary between Afghanistan and then British India (future Pakistan) which he designated through the historical Pashtun tribal area.[35] The boundary was executed disregarding the tribal and ethnic significance, literally splitting villages, tribes, and families arbitrarily. The Russians and British also collaborated in 1897 to establish the northern border. Russian and British policies to further their self interests at the expense of Afghanistan would continue to create problems well into the twentieth century.

Military

Abdur Rahman was a highly talented field commander from an early age, having trained under William Campbell, and was known as General Sher Mohammed Khan after converting to Islam during his youth.[36] He successfully commanded armies under his father, Mohammed Afzal Khan. His first victory as Amir was against the hero of the Second Anglo-Afghan War, Mohammed Ayub Khan, the "Victor of Maiwand," in 1881.[37] Over the course of his twenty year rule, the military conducted eighteen operations to quash revolts and subjugate the tribes throughout Afghanistan.[38] This included the forcible relocation of the Ghilzai tribe, the subjugation of the northern ethnic tribes, and the forced conversion to Islam of Kafiristan (renamed Nuristan).[39] He executed this strategy with the objective of breaking down the tribal system and replacing it with one nation under one law and one ruler. The most important part of his military system was that it was professionally trained and centrally controlled by him. The Army recruited young boys from non-Pashtun families as well as slave boys from areas forcibly subjugated.[40] This included regional armies controlled by the regional governor, who often was a military officer appointed by the Amir. Still, some of his forces had to be provided by tribal levies.[41] Abdur Rahman required tribal leaders to produce one fighting man per seven families, but never depended upon these forces in order to maintain his power or that of Afghanistan.

Economic

Economics were not the strong suit of Abdur Rahman's reign. The most significant portion of the treasury was the annual stipend provided by Great Britain. Subject to resources or high priority political issues, economic reforms were initiated. With the assistance of technicians and experts provided by Great Britain he was able to introduce essential communications, printing firms, and his most important achievement, a small arms factory.[42] The Amir supported the development of small-scale manufacturing involving leather works, medicine, automobiles, and telegraphs.[43] The assistance of French and English engineers introduced modern mining methods regarding copper and lead, as well as a mint that produced up to 10,000 rupees a day.[44]

Social

Abdur Rahman understood the diversity of the Afghanistan ethnic tribes and the Russian-British tensions as the core of Afghanistan's problems. He identified Islam as a common thread between Afghans around which he could build the consensus and cooperation necessary to rule.[45] In order to gain legitimacy in Islam, Abdur Rahman established himself at the spiritual (Imam) leader of Afghanistan (with the corresponding title of "*Millat*").[46] The argument for justification of his role as an Islamic Imam was that it was "Allah who appoints kings and he is ruled by his divine guidance." As an Imam he also secured the role of calling jihad, interpreting Shari'a law and the administration of religious endowments.[47] Although invoking Islam to expel foreign "infidels" had been regularly successful, the notion of solidifying the internal government based on Islam only was not.[48] The system that invoked loyalty and action on a daily basis was at the tribe. Abdur Rahman, the grandson of Dost Mohammed and a Pashtun from the Durrani tribe understood that to effectively rule Afghanistan he must find ways to prevent the fractious tribal system. To this end, Abdur Rahman built the provincial government systems with the thought of replacing the tribal system enough in order to allow him to effectively rule.[49]

Summary

Abdur Rahman Khan was an effective ruler of Afghanistan because he developed a strong national military that stabilized the country. He reduced his reliance upon tribal and religious leaders and co-opted the supreme council (Loya Jirga) that supported Afghan nationalism. He created an effective bureaucracy of civil administrators that reduced the geographical aspects of Afghanistan and extended his control to the rural areas. He was able to maintain foreign relations with Russia and Great Britain that prevented future invasions, although he was unsuccessful in gaining independent control of Afghanistan's international policy or in the establishment of the nation's international borders.

He developed a strong national military that provided him the capability to govern all of Afghanistan. He spent twenty years subjugating unruly tribes in order to provide the stability required for the central government to rule. Although he was still forced to maintain use of the tribal levy system, the vast majority of his military was professional and centrally controlled.

Abdur Rahman Khan believed in Afghan nationalism, that Afghans should be governed under one leader as one people and common goals, not a collection of individual tribes with multiple factions. He understood that Islam was the common bond that connected all of the people of Afghanistan; therefore he utilized that principle successfully by reducing the power and influence of the mullahs and elevating his status as the ruler under the principles of Islam. He further reduced the influence of tribal leaders when he established provincial boundaries and assigned provincial governors supported by the military. This allowed him to consolidate and maintain power without the interference of individual tribal or religious agendas.

Abdur Rahman Khan extended his influence into the rural tribal areas of Afghanistan enough to govern when he developed an effective bureaucracy of civil administrators that supported his provincial governors. A centrally controlled and loyal military supported and sustained this system of a combined central and provincial government.

Abdur Rahman Khan understood that Afghanistan was trapped between the ambitions of both Russia and Great Britain and was not powerful enough to sustain a protracted effort from either. Therefore he focused his efforts on maintaining stability inside of Afghanistan which prevented a vacuum that would entice either country to act. Although Great Britain provided his regime with economic support and control of its foreign policy he maintained a non-provocative policy regarding Russia. His strategy prevented innovation of Afghanistan by Russia or Great Britain but could not prevent either country from interfering with the international borders of Afghanistan, the results of which are still being dealt with today.

The analysis of the regime of Abdur Rahman Khan shows that it is essential to establish a strong military controlled by the central government in order to create stability. Abdur Rahman utilized that military to support his government's efforts to extend services (justice, economic, social) to rural Afghanistan. Additionally he fostered Afghan nationalism by unifying the individual and fractured tribes around the basic principles of an Islamic monarchy but reducing the influence of religious or tribal leaders. Although he was unable to prevent unwanted foreign influence in the affairs of Afghanistan he was able to prevent foreign invasion by controlling what happened within Afghanistan's borders.

Thus, analysis of Abdur Rahman's regime demonstrates that a strong centrally controlled military can create internal stability, prevent foreign invasion, and directly or indirectly support the delivery of government to the rural areas of Afghanistan.

Section II: King Amanullah

The regime of King Amanullah (1919-1929), the "Reformer King," marked the true beginning of independence for Afghanistan by winning control of the nation's foreign policy by waging the Third Anglo-Afghan War.[50] His personal disdain and mistrust for the British resulted in a close political relationship with the newly formed Soviet Union, but also provided Great Britain a reason to oppose his administration.[51] A true progressive, he boldly engaged in a program of modernization through attempting educational, social, religious, and political reforms guided by his mentor and father-in-law, Mahmoud Tarzi. In the end his efforts to implement reforms failed due to his lack of military power and loss of legitimacy with the tribal chiefs and religious mullahs. His positive legacy was establishing and implementing control of Afghanistan's international policy after the successful Third Anglo-Afghan War and belief in a secular liberal democratic government under a constitutional monarchy. His negative legacy was the inability to develop a strong national military or political coalition in order to provide sufficient internal stability to rule, let alone implement reforms, resulting in the popular revolt that led to his overthrow.

Governance

According to Saikal, upon accepting the monarchy on 28 February 1919, Amanullah began his campaign for reform. His acceptance speech, called the "Royal Manifesto," stated:

1. Afghanistan must become free and independent and must enjoy all rights that all other sovereign nations possess.

2. You will help me with all your strength to avenge the blood of the martyr, my deceased father.

3. The nation must become free; no man should be an object of oppression and tyranny.[52]

In doing this Amanullah became the first Afghan ruler to seek legitimacy in the public as opposed to the tribal or religious setting. His hunger for nationalism and modernism led him to seek a military confrontation with Great Britain. In April 1919 at the Grand Mosque in Kabul, Amanullah called for jihad as the crowd shouted "death or freedom."[53] Supported by his two closest advisers, Mahmud Tarzi and General Mohammed Nadir Khan, Amanullah ordered the attack and Afghan forces won early victories. Initially caught off guard, British forces recovered and produced a stalemate when they introduced air power and bombed Jalalabad and Kabul.[54] On 8 August 1919, the British recognized Afghanistan's independence and its right to conduct its own international affairs by signing the Treaty of Rawalpindi.[55] Afghanistan immediately began to exercise its new found international diplomacy. The newly formed Soviet Union was the first country to recognize Afghanistan and they in turn were the first neighbor to recognize the Soviet Union.[56] Moscow immediately offered financial and military aid which was followed up by the 1921 Good Neighbor Treaty and the 1922 Nonaggression Treaty.

Starting in 1919 all the way through 1922, Afghan diplomats traveled through North America, Europe, and the Middle East in order to establish diplomatic relationships and make friendly overtures; they were successful in each nation that they visited except for their main target, the United States.[57] US President Warren Harding received the Afghan mission and promised to consider diplomatic relations but the US government did not positively follow-up. The Afghans were hoping for international support from a nation like the US, which had the military infrastructure and economic strength to provide substantial support, but was physically distant enough so as not to infringe upon its borders. The loss of this opportunity left the Afghans with few choices. The United States concerned about Afghanistan's stability and ties with the Soviets, did not officially recognize the nation of Afghanistan until 1934.[58]

Diplomatic relations with countries in the Middle East and Europe were more successful for Afghanistan.[59] The regime made significant ties with Turkey, Persia, and Egypt in the Middle East, actually gaining strong support from Turkey in the form of military advisers, teachers, and medical as well as scientific training. Amanullah and Tarzi had special admiration for the Turkish leader and a secular-based government.

In Europe, the regime was again well received in Germany, France, and Italy, receiving full recognition and diplomatic relations as well as moderate financial, political, and technical aid. Although there were mutual overtures with Germany, the strategic situation involving both Russia and Great Britain prevented any such relationship materializing. Once again, Afghanistan was left with the option of garnering the support of one or the other.

Relations with the Soviet Union did not go smoothly. Although the Soviets promised substantial financial and political support with no strings attached, they did not have the economic or industrial capacity to deliver all that they promised. Also, Soviet military operations to suppress Islamic militants (known as the "Basmachi" in Russia) inside their own borders often spilled over into Afghanistan, eventually causing political, military, and religious problems for the regime. The fact that the Soviets were a communist nation that was actively oppressing parts of its internal Muslim population was upsetting to the mullahs. Relations with Great Britain were worse and Amanullah refused to take steps to improve them.[60] Additionally, Great Britain was also concerned with unrest in India connected to Islamic militants and Amanullah's possible support.

In 1921, while the reform effort was in full gear under the veil of an anticorruption campaign, Amanullah held a Loya Jirga in order to develop a strategy to combat corruption, the result being "The Basic Codes of the High State of Afghanistan."[61] The codes became the basis for the constitution. With the 1923 Constitution, Amanullah attempted to create a secular state with a constitutional monarchy (based upon the 1906 Persian model), provide equal rights to all ethnic peoples, end the system of slavery, and include rights for women and non-Muslims.[62] He wasted no time in attempting to implement the reform and is known to have disregarded the advice of his two closest advisors, Tarzi and Nadir Shah. Amanullah called a Loya Jirga to review the constitution after being pressured by tribal and religious leaders. Instead of slowing down the pace of his reforms, he began to issue decrees to address them. These events preceded the 1924 Kost rebellion by Pashtun tribesman.[63] The rebellion was suppressed a year later and served as an omen of what was to come.

In 1925, Amanullah's mentor Tarzi resigned. At the same time the Persian government had been overthrown by the secular reformist, Reza Shah who was currently imposing modernization.[64] As part of the reform, men were ordered to wear top hats and women were ordered to remove their veils. Reza Shah "commanded a strong army and a subservient centralized bureaucracy."[65] The fact of the strong army and centralized bureaucracy were key points that escaped Amanullah. Additionally, both Turkey and Persia were focused upon consolidating their internal power and not supporting the global Islamist movement. This left Afghanistan without a dependable international partner.[66] In 1927, King Amanullah and Queen Soroya went on their world tour to all the capitals in Europe, the Middle East, and Asia. The tour served to solidify in his mind the need for immediate installation of his reforms upon his return to Afghanistan.[67]

Upon his return, the King called an immediate Loya Jirga in Kabul and presented the details of his reforms that included not only educational, social, political, and economic modernization, and equality for women, but also the wearing of top hats by men and the removal of the veil by women. Queen Soroya and one hundred women accompanying her removed their veils in the presence of the tribal leaders and mullahs.[68] For the tribal and religious leaders this represented the last straw. King Amanullah's enemies, led predominantly by anti-Amanullah and British supporters, immediately began to actively seek his overthrow. By November of 1928 there was open rebellion in the south, by January of 1929 the king fled his capital Kabul, and by March 1929 the king was exiled in Italy.

Military

King Amanullah initially had the support of the military and its generals including Mohammed Nadir Khan of the Musahiban tribe. His call for jihad and victory in the Third Anglo-Afghan War gave him legitimacy in the eyes of the Afghan Army.[69] After winning the war, Amanullah immersed himself in pursuing diplomatic relations with the international community and implementing reforms in Afghanistan, but his fatal flaw was trying to implement a "large-scale program of reform without a strong and well-trained army and a loyal and disciplined bureaucracy."[70] In 1921, Amanullah began his modernization of the military under the advice of Tarzi and Turkish military advisers.[71] His immediate aim was to make it smaller but more professional and efficient; what actually happened was a twenty-five percent pay reduction, a purge of senior officers and veteran units, and closure of the military academy. By 1924, the address system changed and altered the ultimate size and function of the Army. Military pay and life was severely substandard and the Army became nonfunctional for anyone to see.[72] Eventually Amanullah scrapped the modernization plans and training was replaced with an educational program. He reduced the size of the Army to 23,010 and finally to a low of 11,000.[73] A variety of military equipment from different countries sat rusting due to lack of maintenance, repair parts, and trained personnel necessary to operate it. Corruption at all levels aggravated these problems.[74]

Economic

Initially King Amanullah concentrated on his relationship with the Soviet Union, hoping that support from the Russians would make up the loss of revenue from Great Britain. The King secured foreign aid agreements from the Soviet Union and received aid as early as 1919.[75] The initial gifts included thirteen airplanes supported by mechanics, pilots, and air routes from Moscow to Kabul. Later the Soviets built telephone lines and roads, while the Germans built the only rail line in Afghanistan. The monetary aid from Great Britain ended after the Third Anglo-Afghan War; the King's negative attitude towards Great Britain assured that they would not support him economically unless it was to strategically blunt the Soviet Union.

Development of the 1923 Constitution allowed the King to focus upon economic reforms inside of Afghanistan. King Amanullah's financial reforms were based upon infrastructure development, reorganizing tax and fiscal systems, broadening opportunities in land ownership, and replacing the old currency (rupee) with a new unit (afghani).[76] The most lasting effects from the reforms were in land ownership. Due to the reforms, landless peasant farmers were provided the opportunity to purchase land from the monarchy at reasonable prices. Traditional land ownership left the vast majority of land in the hands of the monarchy, tribal leaders, the tribal community, or religious endowment.

The reforms concerning infrastructure had more mixed results. Clearly important projects were undertaken and completed including roads, telephone lines, as well as government and industrial structures but many of the structures proved to be lavish expenditures and contributed to the overspending of the budget. One area where the government saved money was in military spending. The military budget was slashed and the standing army severely downsized in order to fund many of the progressive reform projects. The last major spending project of the administration was construction of the new capital built just six miles outside of Kabul. "Dar'ul Aman" was the selected name of the new capital and it included a royal palace as well as the parliament building. The overly excessive spending habits of the Amanullah regime combined with a weak military and significantly underpaid civil administrators and bureaucrats left the King with an administration that could not govern effectively.[77]

Social

King Amanullah began his regime with strong legitimacy founded on Islamic principles and nationalism through his call for jihad against Great Britain in order for Afghanistan to exercise its rights of full independence.[78] King Amanullah quickly squandered this advantage with his radical reform agenda which alienated military, tribal leaders, and the conservative mullahs. The reforms were clearly well-meaning, developed to support the rights of women and ethnic minorities, with the intent of supporting a modernization of Afghanistan and moving it towards a secular democracy. Having been inspired by the success of such movements in Turkey and Persia, the King disregarded the advice of not only his advisers but also that of his grandfather Abdur Rahman, the Iron Amir. [79] Although there was significant opposition to the reforms themselves, clearly the pace of change was also a key factor in their failure. Many of the reforms were simply announced by King Amanullah in the form of a decree and would not be heard of outside of the city of Kabul for months, normally reaching the rural areas in the form of rumors. This simply armed King Amanullah's detractors with additional issues to weaken his political power.

The catastrophic event that destroyed the social contract between King Amanullah and the people of Afghanistan was his 1928 world tour.[80] From the beginning of his trip, the King received negative press reports back in Afghanistan. Photographs of Queen Soroya in Europe unveiled and wearing inappropriate Western styled clothes in both formal and casual environments were circulated throughout Afghanistan, angering mullahs and giving the commoners reasons to doubt the King's piety and judgment.[81] When upon his return in July 1928, he convened a Loya Jirga and announced a sweeping program of reforms, the mullahs decided to act -- calling for a jihad to overthrow the king to restore Islamic rule, thus paving the way for the ultimate rebellion which ended his regime.[82]

The analysis of the social environment of Afghanistan during the reign of King Amanullah illuminates the tension that can exist between the central government and the tribal and religious communities when liberal progressive reforms are forcibly implemented. Clearly the examples displayed by Turkey describe how the exact same reforms can be implemented when done deliberately and thoughtfully after having first developed a strong professional military and a large and effective civil administrative bureaucracy.

Summary

King Amanullah was ultimately unsuccessful in modernizing or governing Afghanistan because he failed to develop a national military that could maintain internal stability. He failed to establish support or acceptance of his progressive social and economic reforms by the people of Afghanistan, and lost power and influence to tribal leaders and Islamic mullahs. He failed to maintain or support an effective civil administration capable of delivering governmental services to the tribal people of rural Afghanistan. Although he successfully secured full independence and total control of Afghanistan and its foreign policy, he unwisely antagonized Great Britain and openly courted the Soviet Union creating an equally chaotic international situation to complement the chaotic internal situation in Afghanistan.

King Amanullah did not simply fail to develop a national military. He functionally dismantled and ultimately destroyed the Afghan military. He did this by actively ignoring the advice given to him by his closest advisers, Minister of Defense, General Nadir Shah, and even his late grandfather Abdur Rahman. Without a strong military he was unable to maintain the internal stability necessary to implement his reforms or maintain control over rebellious tribal leaders and Islamic mullahs.

King Amanullah aggressively established and attempted to implement a full range of progressive social and economic reforms. He had hoped to establish a constitutional monarchy in Afghanistan that respected the rights of ethnic minorities, women, and all religions. He failed to realize that such a broad range of reforms required in equally broad base of support such as internal stability, an educated population, support from tribal and religious leaders, and effective bureaucratic system to implement it. Without any of these support mechanisms his reform agenda acted in a way that accelerated his downfall from power, resulting in a civil rebellion that the weak national army could not repel.

King Amanullah allowed the once functional civil administration of the Afghanistan government to become an effective and plagued by corruption. He was not able to build the additional capability to maintain or extend government control or influence beyond the national or provincial capital cities to the tribal areas in rural Afghanistan. His regime became isolated physically, politically, and socially. Rumors and speculation replaced accurate information regarding government activities, often to the detriment of the regime.

King Amanullah succeeded in establishing Afghan and foreign policy regarding the broader international community and establishing relations with Arabic, European, and Asian countries with whom they had formerly been isolated from but he failed to establish the key relationships with nations such as United States that had the sufficient economic, political, and military influence necessary to support Afghanistan. Ultimately he openly played his relationship with the Soviet Union in a way that continually antagonized Great Britain and angered Afghan tribal as well as religious leaders. Although the Soviet Union provided significant financial support, they could not have the economic capability or political will to fully support Afghanistan and eventually became more concerned with repressing their internal Islamic militants.

The analysis of King Amanullah's failed regime explains much. His failure to develop a strong centrally controlled military was the key factor in his inability to maintain stability and implement necessary progressive reforms, and resulted in his overthrow by civil revolt. His failure to maintain and grow the capability of the government civil administration combined with the loss of support from tribal and religious leaders resulted in his regime being physically, politically, and socially isolated. With no viable dependable international partner, his regime was also internationally isolated. The situation eventually left the future of Afghanistan in the hands of the tribal leaders and the Islamic mullahs.

The key lessons that could be taken away from King Amanullah's regime were that the inability to development a strong centrally controlled military led to internal instability and also contributed to the unsuccessful implementation of his reforms. Additionally, failure to build or maintain an effective civil administrative bureaucracy led to the physical, political, and social internal isolation of the regime and prevented it's capability to provide effective government. Finally, international isolation had as devastating an effect as international hyperactivity for Afghanistan.

Section III: Nadir Shah

Nadir Shah (1929-1933) reestablished internal stability and also developed a multidimensional foreign policy that included both Great Britain and the Soviet Union. Unlike the idealist Amanullah, Nadir was pragmatic and understood the necessity of rebuilding and modernizing the military before forcing liberal reforms. Nadir quickly and efficiently rebuilt and revitalized the Afghanistan military structure which he used to stabilize the country.[83] Furthermore the reforms that he did concentrate on were more economic based reforms, which he implemented to stimulate the economy of Afghanistan and reduce the foreign influence over their internal economy.[84] He also understood the conservative Afghanistan culture and was able to gain legitimacy as well as the cooperation of the tribal chiefs and religious mullahs. Nadir dealt quickly and harshly with his detractors and those who were uncooperative. He used the 1931 Constitution to consolidate his power by establishing political coalitions involving his family members, close allies, as well as tribal and religious leaders.[85] Although his reign was short, he was able to establish the foundations that would last for forty years. His positive legacy was quickly reestablishing and creating balance in all elements of national power and creating a functional political coalition that allowed the central government to rule. His negative legacy was that in order to repair the damage caused by King Amanullah's regime, he had to cede power to the religious mullahs and persecute the supporters of King Amanullah, creating two separate camps instead of a broad coalition.

Governance

The 1931 Constitution displayed the political agenda of Nadir Shah.[86] His purpose was to reunite the people of Afghanistan through the principles of Islam, consolidate his political power that would allow him to govern, and build the foundation for long-term political, military, and economic stability for the people of Afghanistan.[87] Because of the direct role that they had in bringing down the previous regime, Nadir permitted religious leaders more influence than they enjoyed under King Amanullah. Nadir deliberately undid many reforms implemented in the 1923 Constitution and returned Afghanistan to national gradualism in terms of political reforms.[88] Nadir received tremendously valuable support from his brothers and other close allies. Nadir and his family members, the Musahiban, had great influence and understanding with the Pashtun tribes. In September 1930 he called for a Loya Jirga of 286 members.[89] Nadir took a slow, deliberate, and moderate approach to implementing reforms. As he had advised the previous king, he noted that he wanted to implement reforms in Afghanistan and would have to first build a strong and well disciplined loyal military, supported by an efficient bureaucracy. He would also have to implement reforms in such a way as to not alienate the tribal leaders or mullahs. Therefore he prioritized his effort in order to allow him to rule in an effective manner. He also believed it was important to strengthen the economy of Afghanistan in order to provide increased opportunity for the Afghan people.

In the area of foreign policy and international relations, Nadir's top priority was to bring balance to Afghans' interactions with Great Britain and the Soviet Union.[90] As Minister of Defense for the previous administration, he witnessed the chaos caused by alienating one or both of the great powers.

Nadir believed that a balanced approach of neutrality was in the best interest of Afghanistan. In May of 1930 he confirmed the Anglo-Afghan Treaty of 1921, and in 1931 he signed a Treaty of Mutual Neutrality and Nonaggression with the Soviet Union. Nadir was also able to build upon the positive diplomatic relations that had developed during the previous regime with countries in the Middle East, Europe, and Asia; either signing treaties of friendship and cooperation or confirming the ones that already existed. [91]

Military

As a former general in the National Army of Afghanistan as well as a Defense Minister and advisor to the previous regime, Nadir had the experience and expertise to rebuild the national army. These qualities enabled him to properly prioritize the necessary changes and then to skillfully and deliberately execute them. His main priority was to build the army and provide for adequate equipping and proper training. Nadir and his brothers had strong ties and influence with tribal leaders. This combined with his successful campaign during the recent rebellion provided Nadir with the needed legitimacy within the military and tribal communities. Nadir was able to successfully utilize the "*laskar*" system of tribal armies that supported the central government during national emergencies. With no national army at his disposal Nadir was able to establish a fighting force with support from the Pashtun tribes located on both sides of the Durand line. Nadir understood that the tribal system cannot be counted on by a ruler to create or sustain internal stability. Nadir reestablished the national army's military academy in 1930, taking control of the training of future officers as well as establishing a noncommissioned officers training to improve the professionalism inside military ranks, based upon the Turkish army model.[92] The army grew to more than 70,000 troops with modern weapons that far exceeded the combat capabilities of the tribal militias which it proved by successfully putting down multiple revolts over the next ten years.[93]

Economic

The aftermath of the 1929 revolt left the capital city looted and the treasury depleted. The desire to remain neutral in matters concerning the Soviet Union and Great Britain also resulted in the loss of external financial aid and assistance. Nadir would be left with the challenge of revising the economy of Afghanistan without the assistance of the international community. Nadir initiated a series of aggressive and successful economic reforms that ultimately improved a previously stagnant Afghanistan economy. First, through efficiently collecting taxes, Nadir was able to replenish the treasury. He revised the investment system, transforming it into a national banking system which allowed the government as well as individual investors to pursue revenue, as well as successfully forcing investors to fund a draining of swamps in order to turn them into productive land. International trade in the areas of cotton, Afghan rugs, animal furs and skins continued to improve with Russia and Europe. In the area of internal infrastructure, Nadir completed the construction of the North-South Road running through the Hindu Kush from Kabul. The road improvement projects had a positive effect on travel and commerce inside Afghanistan, as well as allowing him the ability to quickly move military forces to and from Kabul. [94]

Social

Tribal leaders and Islamic mullahs immediately forced Nadir to establish legitimacy with them due to the total breakdown of their relationship with Amanullah at the end of his regime. In September 1930, Nadir called together a Loya Jirga in order to establish legitimacy.[95] Nadir used the opportunity to formally roll back many of the unpopular reforms initiated by King Amanullah and established a base of support for his 1931 Constitution. The language used in the Constitution was specifically Islamic and therefore firmly established Afghanistan as an Islamic nation. This was a clear step taken to distinguish his regime from the previous regime. Nadir took additional specific steps to strengthen his relationship with tribal leaders and religious mullahs, as well as subjugate his political enemies.[96] The Pashtun tribes that helped Nadir seize power were exempted from certain taxes as well as tribal levies for the military. Some tribal leaders were given honorary military appointments, and trusted friends and family members were placed in key administrative positions. Nadir was also quick to eliminate his political enemies and quiet dissent. His regressive reform efforts created enemies from the progressive supporters of King Amanullah. The consequences of these harsh measures resulted in the assassinations of Nadir's brother in June 1933 and his own assassination in November 1933.[97] The assassin was a high school student seeking revenge, whose family had been Amanullah supporters and had experienced repression under Nadir. The assassin was subsequently tortured and executed in front of his family to send a message to those planning future attacks on the royal family.

Summary

In only four short years Nadir Shah transformed Afghanistan from a failed state into a constitutional monarchy. Nadir Shah rebuilt the Afghan national military into a strong and modern force that allowed him to create stability within Afghanistan. He co-opted tribal and religious leaders and gain the support of the people by establishing an Islamic Constitution. He reestablished an effective civil demonstration and controlled the by placing family members entrusted tribal affiliates in key positions. He built upon international relationships established for the previous regime and brought balance to relationships concerning the Soviet Union and Great Britain. The newly transformed Afghanistan system of government would survive for 40 more years.

Nadir Shah quickly rebuilt the Afghan military that had been allowed to disintegrate during the previous regime. He modernized military training and equipment and reestablished the military college and noncommissioned officer training. He ended the tribal levy system focused on professionalizing the military. The revitalized military allowed him to stabilize Afghanistan and establish an effective government.

Nadir Shah established legitimacy and gained the support of Pashtun Tribal leaders and Islamic Mullahs. He established an Islamic Constitution and focused his reform effort on economic and not social issues. He allowed supportive tribal and religious leaders some of the influence and power that previous regimes had taken away. Those who refused to support him were dealt with harshly.

Nadir Shah reestablished an effective bureaucratic system of civil administrators that he controlled through family members and trusted tribal affiliates. He uses control of the civilian administrative and military base to extend his authority to rural Afghanistan. He focused his economic and infrastructure projects outside of the major cities and gained legitimacy from people.

Nadir Shah improved overall Afghanistan foreign relations and strengthened Afghanistan's position with the Soviet Union and Great Britain. He continued to build and grow relationships with countries in Europe, Asia, and among the Islamic nations. He balanced Afghanistan's relationships with Great Britain and the Soviet Union. He signed treaties with both nations and at the time of his assassination had stopped relying on foreign aid from either country.

Analysis of the regime of Nadir Shah showed the significance of government control over an effective military and bureaucratic system of civil administrators. Furthermore, it provided insight concerning Afghan culture, based upon his successful process to establish an Islamic Constitution and obtain support from tribal and religious leaders. He used traditional as well as practical means to legitimize his rule and consolidate power. It also proved the value of focused economic reforms and infrastructure improvement that Nadir Shah utilized to extend his government's reach to rural Afghanistan. Finally, the analysis of this regime displayed that Afghanistan established a stable nation with limited foreign international interference or economic aid.

The key take away provided by Nadir Shah is that four years after the total disintegration of the government of Afghanistan he was able to rebuild the military, the government, and legitimacy with the people that resulted in a stabilized the country and foreign relations. The system that he built was the basis of the government and military of Afghanistan that lasted for the next 40 years.

Section IV: Operation Enduring Freedom –
International Security Assistance Force in Afghanistan

The historical case studies of Afghanistan's past regimes can be compared and contrasted with the current US strategy being employed in Afghanistan in order to identify possible lessons learned. The analysis shows similar trends and methods that proved successful for past regimes are currently being employed by the United States and the international coalition. The focus is upon building a well-trained military large enough and properly equipped in order to provide the central government the ability to create stability and internal security required to effectively govern. The coalition is also providing a base for government while helping create legitimacy amongst Afghanistan's people through the process of developing and implementing a constitution while including the historic institution of the Loya Jirga in order to legitimize the process.

There is also the understanding that the central government of Afghanistan lacks the capacity and penetration necessary to provide security and service to the rural Afghan people. Because of this, the Afghan people depend primarily upon their tribe or local community for governance and security. In the absence of a tribal system or when that tribe is weak, then rural Afghans are at the mercy of warlords, criminals, or insurgent groups such as the Taliban.[98] The current government effort is severely lacking and a major impediment to real progress and legitimacy.

The major task is to implement a strong military that is loyal to the central government.[99] A strong military can produce a stable environment that may allow the government the opportunity to provide justice and service to the people. To build a strong and capable military, will require enough money, support, and time to properly develop, train and equip Afghan formations. Without a strong military, the government cannot succeed.

Internationally, Afghanistan is no longer caught in the middle of the "Great Game" between Great Britain and Russia, but in new game involving ISAF, NATO, Pakistan, India, and Iran. Once again, the tribal areas divided by the Durand line along the Afghanistan and Pakistan border are critical. The United States and the international coalition have the potential to assist Afghanistan and help bring order to this area which is currently in chaos. Pakistan is currently the safe-haven afforded Taliban insurgents who launch attacks from the tribal areas bordering Afghanistan. If ISAF and NATO successfully develop an approach that denies the insurgents this safe-haven and addresses Pakistan's concerns, it has the potential of tipping the scale dramatically.

The international community must also deal with the long-term economic and diplomatic situation facing Afghanistan. At some point there must be economic and diplomatic decisions and policies developed that address future engagement necessary to provide Afghanistan the strategic time and space needed to develop the capability required to penetrate into rural areas and provide effective governance to the people of Afghanistan. There is also the need to understand and respect the Afghan culture and implement any necessary reforms in a responsible manner that does not overwhelm the social or political environment, but that also abides by international laws and respects human rights.

Governance

In 2002 after the defeat of the Taliban, the international community under the Bonn Agreement established the Afghanistan Transitional Authority (ATA). Hamid Karzai became the interim President of Afghanistan, and the International Security Assistance Force in Afghanistan (ISAF) was authorized.[100] Significant to this process was the "emergency" Loya Jirga convened 11-19 June 2002 (1,600 delegates), at which Hamid Karzai's appointment received legitimacy in the traditional Afghan manner.[101] The same process took place after the development of the 2004 Constitution of the Islamic Republic of Afghanistan, and the Berlin Conference in which the international community pledged economic aid. In 2008 at the Paris conference, the international community established the Afghanistan National Development Strategy (ANDS) which established as its goal to create a "stable Islamic democracy by 2020."[102] The international community has not matched rhetoric with commitment, either with the required economic aid or the dedicated security forces, political support, and development of the mission on the ground.

National elections for the presidency of Afghanistan took place in August 2009 with mixed results. President Hamid Karzai was eventually declared the winner although there was substantiated election fraud as well as violence from the Taliban and insurgent groups. The incident left international observers and the Obama administration cautious of President Karzai's capability to lead the government and combat the increasing corruption within the floundering government. The new US strategy demands a committed partner and Afghanistan's history demands a talented ruler.

Military

General McChrystal quickly established his intent of refocusing ISAF and NATO forces on protecting the population of Afghanistan and not upon killing the insurgents.[103] The new guidance changed the way operations were conducted throughout the operational environment. Restrictions were placed on the use of close air support and indirect fire in order to reduce and eliminate the number of civilian non-combatants killed or injured by coalition forces. There was also an increased focus upon building the capability of the Afghanistan government to deliver services to the isolated rural populations, normally outside of the reach of the weak central government. ISAF and NATO forces employed Provincial Reconstruction Teams (PRTs) which utilized funds provided under the Commander's Emergency Response Program (CERP) in order to meet the needs of rural Afghans.[104] US PRTs are mainly manned by military personnel with a minimal number of State Department members, but the increased troop surge announcements include civilian State Department and US Agency for International Development (USAID) personnel.[105]

On 1 May 2002, President George W. Bush announced that the US military would begin training the new Afghan National Army (ANA). The 3rd Special Forces Group was assigned the mission of creating an ethnically integrated national military.[106] This announcement represented the fourth time that Afghanistan had embarked upon rebuilding its national army.[107] On 21 November 2009, NATO Training Mission – Afghanistan (NTM-A) joined with Combined Security Transitioned Command – Afghanistan (CSTC-A), to include the creation of the Combined Training Advisory Group - Police (CTAG-P), all under the command of Lieutenant General William B. Caldwell, IV.[108]

The Afghanistan National Army (ANA) receives large numbers of quality recruits; the goal is 305,000 personnel (400,000 under consideration). The seven Commando Brigades are outstanding and operate with SOF. The ANA development is focused in three areas; recruiting /training, professional development, and institutional development. Leader development is top priority with emphasis in the area of combined operations and transition to Afghans in the lead. Air Corps has good training results and is being used consistently during operations. The MI-17 helicopter is perfect for Afghanistan terrain, but short in total numbers. There are some problems retaining pilots. They sometimes go AWOL while in the states, or quit to get civilian jobs after trained. Further, there are major maintenance problems with the helicopters. The ANA requires 1,300 additional instructors and institutional combined arms training. Afghanistan National Police (ANP) casualty rate is four times greater than army. There is no ANP training academy in country; international training is conducted in Jordan, India, and Turkey.[109]

The Afghanistan Security Forces are collocated with the five ISAF Regional Commands.[110] The five Regional Commands consist of the following: Regional Command Capital (RC Capital) is controlled by France, the ANA 201 Corps and the Afghan Air Corps located at Kabul. Regional Command East (RC East) is controlled by the United States located at Bagram, and the ANA 203 Corps located at Gardez. Regional Command South (RC South) is controlled by The Netherlands out of Tarin Kowt, and the ANA 205 Corps located at Kandahar. Regional Command West (RC West) is controlled by Italy and the ANA 207 Corps collocated out of Heart. Regional Command North (RC North) is controlled by Germany from Konduz, and the ANA 209 out of Mazar-e-Sharif. The ISAF current strength is approximately 102,500 troops from forty-six contributing nations. The ANA strength is approximately 93,980 soldiers.[111]

Most of the major insurgent groups in Afghanistan fight in the eastern and southern regions taking refuge across the Pakistan border.[112] The Quetta Shura Taliban, led by Mullah Omar operates throughout RC South in Helmand, Kandahar, and Zabul Provinces. The Haqqani Network, led by Jalaluddin and Sirajuddin Haqqani operate throughout RC East, including Kabul. Hizb-e Islami Gulbuddin led by Gulbuddin Hekmatyar also operates within RC East, including the Khyber Pass. Also operating from the same safe havens are insurgent groups focused upon attacking Pakistan. These groups include Tehrik-e Talliban-e Pakistan, Lashkar-e Tayyiba, and Terik-e Nafaz-e Shariat-e. These insurgent groups are believed to be providing protection to Osama bin Laden and the Al-Qaeda Network. [113]

Economic

Afghanistan's economic problem is that the majority of its economy (66%) is either foreign aid, mainly provided by the United States government, or money derived from the illicit drug trade involving the production and distribution of heroin originating in the poppy fields of Afghanistan. The Afghanistan gross domestic product (GDP) is estimated at $9.8 billion; $3 billion international aid, $3 billion trade and commerce, and $3 billion production and distribution of illegal drugs.[114] Afghanistan will have to develop economic markets and industries that provide opportunities for its people and international drug trade will have to be contained and reduced. Afghanistan will require continued economic support from the international community and the United States government until the security situation can be stabilized and allow unopposed economic growth.

Since 2001 the United States has provided more than $38 billion to Afghanistan, with more than 60% being provided since 2007. The Obama Administration requested nearly $12 billion from Congress for use in Afghanistan in 2010.[115] A successful counterinsurgency campaign that provides security and allows the Afghan government to build the capacity needed to provide services will create the conditions conducive to entice international investment. Foreign investments will be necessary to replace large portions of foreign aid and fuel economic growth in Afghanistan.

Afghanistan has been and remains an agriculturally based economy with more than 80% of the population involved in farming on top of a 40% unemployment rate.[116] The US State Department and coalition allies work with the Afghan government to rebuild the agricultural structure of Afghanistan. The NATO and ISAF PRTs are the lead organizations charged with providing local communities and villagers in rural Afghanistan access to the limited funds, programs, and technology available to improve their situation.[117] This method of accessing, obtaining, and delivering goods and services to rural Afghans has earned legitimacy and built trust.[118] The trust and legitimacy lead to increased information gathering and sharing, this leads to increased understanding of the population's problems, which allows coalition forces the opportunity to solve them. The end result is increased security and a more stable environment.

Social

ISAF and NATO counterinsurgency (COIN) strategy and the development and training of the Afghanistan Security Forces, have considered, respected, and co-opted many key aspects of the Afghanistan culture and traditions. In COIN operations, information gathering, information sharing, the employment of PRTs, the use of security sector reforms (SSRs), and implementation of the judicial system are all examples of ISAF and the coalition allies leveraging of the Afghan culture in order to build trust and deliver results. Within the Afghan National Military system the ethnically-conscious recruiting, development, and training of the army is essential as well as historically significant. The recognition and proper utilization of culturally significant forms of legitimacy, such as the "Loya Jirga or Arbakai," can prove to be effective points of departure or missed opportunities. The coalition counterinsurgency strategy has the opportunity to create synergy when it can leverage these cultural systems, traditions, and situations.

The collection and sharing of information is a key element of the ISAF and NATO counterinsurgency strategy, and the basis of a successful coalition intelligence effort. As part of the necessity to change the focus from killing insurgents to protecting the Afghan people a number of distinctions must be made in order to collect and use the right information as well as ensure that it is widely shared and distributed to the right people. ISAF and NATO Commander General Stanley McChrystal has supported and established this new way of collecting intelligence within the subordinate commands in Afghanistan.[119] General McChrystal believed that changing the system was imperative for two important reasons; one is that "senior leaders at the highest levels are making important decisions based on the information collected, that information should make its way from the sensor to the decision maker." Second, the most important information that is needed to protect the population is information about the population, not the enemy. "White intelligence" (population based information) provides coalition forces the details of what problems the population is facing and therefore the problems ISAF and NATO should be addressing.[120]

In order to further this effort, General McChrystal and Lieutenant General David Rodriguez, Commander of the ISAF Joint Command, have advocated and supported "community information centers." These community information centers have been set up at regional command locations and maximize the use of unclassified open source information with a focus on "host nation information." This method is in synch with the overall ISAF and NATO counterinsurgency strategy and therefore receives great support by the Commanding Generals.[121] The information gathered and shared assists units, PRTs, government officials and tribal or community leaders, which in turn allows coalition and Afghan security forces the means to successfully achieve goals and accomplish missions.

Summary

The United States and the international coalition are conducting an aggressive counterinsurgency strategy in order to protect the people of the Islamic Republic of Afghanistan, develop the Afghan National Security Forces, assist the government of Afghanistan in the effort to build capacity and deliver services to the people of rural Afghanistan, and address the regional conflicts involving Pakistan, India, and Iran, that will allow Afghanistan to secure its external borders. Officially the coalition is operating within an eighteen month timeframe before the coalition nations including the United States begin to reduce combat troop levels. Coalition commanders and their staffs must deal with the problem of how to generate the desired effects and secure objectives along the current lines of effort within the current timeframe.

NATO and ISAF forces are successfully developing a security system in Afghanistan that includes a national army, air force, and police force. The Afghan national military development includes command and control as well as logistical organizations. Training includes basic training, officer and noncommissioned officer training, including a four year military academy. Currently aviation and police training are conducted outside of Afghanistan; long term plans are to correct that situation. The long term success or failure of the Afghan Security Forces is an essential factor regarding the success or failure of the Islamic Republic of Afghanistan.

NATO and ISAF are utilizing human terrain teams (HTT) and provincial reconstruction teams (PRT) within the context of counterinsurgency strategy in order to understand the cultural environment and better support the government of Afghanistan build capacity and deliver services to the Afghan people. President Hamid Karzai has established an Islamic Constitution and utilized the system of *loya jirga* as traditional means to establish legitimacy. The president's leadership and ability to establish an effective government have been called into question due to fraud in the recent presidential elections as well as continued corruption within his administration. Yet his Pashtun tribal ties may provide him an opportunity to reconcile some moderate Taliban elements and co-opt their support.

NATO and ISAF have also surged civil administrators, State Department personnel, and agricultural experts in order to build the government of Afghanistan's capacity to support its population. Historically, absence of a strong central government empowered the independent Afghan tribes that could provide the needed security and prosperity to care for the people. The harsh terrain and poor infrastructure of roads and highways tended to allow the Afghan tribes to conduct their business without interference. Today, Afghanistan's weak central government must build greater capacity in order to support a tribal system weakened by thirty years of war, poverty, and assaults from the Taliban, Al-Qaeda, narcotic traffickers, and warlords. The critical problem concerning the government of Afghanistan is its ability to build capacity within the current strategic timeline of the United States and the international coalition.

The US State Department and coalition diplomats are attempting to create working solutions in order to stabilize regional security surrounding Afghanistan, with emphasis on the international border between Afghanistan and Pakistan. Until the Taliban insurgents can be dealt with on both sides of the border the insurgency will not likely be militarily contained. In this situation international assistance is critical to the security of Afghanistan. Additionally, Afghanistan will require sustained economic support from the international community for the foreseeable future.

Analysis of the ongoing NATO and ISAF campaign shows an effort in developing the Afghanistan Security Forces and executing counterinsurgency strategy, the success of which will create the time and space necessary to build the capacity of the government of the Islamic Republic of Afghanistan. Although President Karzai, an ethnic Pashtun, established an Islamic Constitution and has utilized traditional Afghan methods to establish legitimacy, he has not yet been able to successfully transform this into the political influence necessary to successfully produce an effective government in Afghanistan. The coalition partners have identified the necessity of addressing the regional security concerns of Pakistan, but that will be a long term ongoing process. The international community must continue to commit to the long term economic and diplomatic support required to transform Afghanistan.

Conclusion

The conflict in Afghanistan may ultimately be summarized as a battle between the strength of the United States' strategy of counterinsurgency and the ability of NATO and ISAF to produce a stable government, thus allowing the United States and the international community to disengage from major combat operations, entrusting the day-to-day security of Afghanistan to the Afghanistan security forces. NATO and ISAF forces find themselves engaged in this conflict not simply against the Taliban or the forces of Al-Qaeda but against the holistic operational environment of Afghanistan which includes an historical and cultural regional context that has lasted more than three hundred years. The key factor to success or failure in Afghanistan will be its ability to develop an effective government that can produce the necessary security that will provide the stability to enable the government to deliver the services necessary to allow Afghanistan to develop and grow as an independent nation. The Afghanistan National Security Forces (National Military, National Police) are the keys to extending the government's penetration into the rural areas of Afghanistan in order to provide government to the people of Afghanistan.

The historical analysis of Afghanistan suggests that for Afghanistan to succeed as a nation it must have a central government, led by a strong legitimate leader, and supported by a strong and loyal military. The military creates the stability necessary for the government to govern the Afghan people through the delivery of security and justice. For the government to survive, the military must be loyal to the ruler or ruling coalition. Afghanistan has historically been led by Pashtun rulers since 1747 with only one exception.[122] The successful rulers somehow managed to co-opt tribal and religious leaders and gain their support.

The situation facing NATO and ISAF when viewed through an historical backdrop would indicate that the current effort in building a large, capable security force is the key if not decisive factor. The speed and efficiency in developing a well-trained, well-led, well-equipped and self-sustaining security force over the next twelve to eighteen months will indicate whether Afghanistan will be poised to succeed or not. Historically, no Afghan ruler or regime has proven otherwise. Based upon the current training results that show continuing progress, Afghanistan could be poised to move forward. The key unknown is whether Afghan President Hamid Karzai is the strong Pashtun leader capable of commanding the loyalty of the military, tribal, and religious leaders necessary to govern Afghanistan.

The current NATO and ISAF counterinsurgency strategy is presently providing the strategic time and space necessary to build capability in the security forces as well as the government of the Islamic Republic of Afghanistan. History indicates that victory in Afghanistan will have to be an Afghan process. At some point, an Afghan leader legitimate in the eyes of the people must utilize the Afghan military and take back his country from the insurgents. NATO and ISAF must continue to provide time and space, rapidly build capability in the military and government, and focus on the inevitable transition of authority that must happen in order to succeed. At that point President Karzai or someone else must be ready willing and able to take that responsibility.

Every Afghan hamlet located near the Afghanistan – Pakistan border is part of the newest version of "The Great Game."[123] This new version 2.0 is the lethal competition to win the loyalty or subjugation of the people. Afghans at the lowest level are forced to choose between an absent, incompetent government or an always present but vicious and backward Taliban. For the Taliban the rules are simple: There are no rules. The Taliban will do whatever works today as long as it gives them power and influence. For the coalition the rules are equally simple: Protect the people long enough to allow the nation of Afghanistan to develop the capacity and the will to provide enough government in the forms of security, justice, economic, and social reform. The game will be fought in the rugged and unforgiving terrain of Afghanistan, but it will ultimately be decided inside the equally complex and unforgiving "human terrain" of the Afghan tribes.[124] History has indicated that the key factor required for a successful national government is a large, capable and loyal military, led by a strong, legitimate leader.

Comparison of the coalition analysis against the context of Afghanistan's history has indicated that NATO and ISAF should continue to develop the security forces of Afghanistan while continuing to assist President Karzai in establishing an effective government capable of command and control of the military in order to stabilize Afghanistan. The government of the Islamic Republic of Afghanistan must establish trust and legitimacy between itself and the people through the delivery of security, justice, economic opportunity, and governance at the local level. The international community must transition to a position of support that will allow Afghanistan to develop without unnecessary interference.

The key take away concerning the United States and the international coalition is that historically the ability to develop a strong capable Afghan military has been the decisive factor concerning the success or failure of the nation of Afghanistan. The Afghan military and security forces can provide the link that will enable the Afghan government to penetrate rural Afghanistan and deliver the necessary security, justice, and services that the people of Afghanistan require. This is critical because the weakened Afghan tribal system leaves the people of Afghanistan vulnerable to the anti-governmental elements. A strong and powerful military, loyal to the government of the Islamic Republic of Afghanistan is the key factor toward development of Afghanistan national stability.

Notes

1.   White House Interagency Policy Group, "White Paper of the Interagency Policy Group's Report on US Policy Toward Afghanistan and Pakistan," Office of the President, Washington, DC, March 2009, 1-5, http://www.whitehouse.gov/assets/documents/Afghanistan-Pakistan_White_ Paper.pdf   (accessed 9 October 2009).

2.   Kimberly Kagan, "Afghan Army and Police Forces Must Grow Much Larger," *Washington Examiner,* final edition, August 18, 2009.

3.   Kenneth Katzman, "Afghanistan: Post-Taliban Governance, Security, and US Policy," *Congressional Research Service* (March 1, 2010), 29, http://www.fas.org/sgp/crs/row/RL30588. pdf (accessed 1 March 2010).

4.   Commander NATO International Security Assistance Force, Afghanistan, and US Forces, Afghanistan, "Commander's Initial Assessment," August 30, 2009. http://media.washingtonpost. com/wp-srv/politics/documents/Assessment_Redacted_092109.pdf.

5.   Steve Bowman and Catherine Dale, "War in Afghanistan: Strategy, Military Operations, and Issues for Congress," *Congressional Research Service* (February 25, 2010), 31. http://www. fas.org/sgp/crs/natsec/R40156.pdf (accessed 1 March 2010).

6.   Katzman, "Afghanistan: Post-Taliban Governance, Security, and US Policy," 43.

7.   Ali A. Jalali, "Rebuilding Afghanistan's National Army," *Parameters*, Vol.32 (Autumn 2002), 72.

8.   Ali A. Jalali, 72.

9.   Ali A. Jalali, 73.

10.   *CIA - The World Fact Book*, October 5, 2009. https://www.cia.gov/library/publications/ the-world-factbook/geos/af.html (accessed 1 March 2010).

11.   *CIA - The World Fact Book.*

12.   *Institute for the Study of War*, October 9, 2009. http://www.understandingwar.org/ afghanistan-project/maps (accessed 1 March 2010).

13.   Ali A. Jalali, "Winning in Afghanistan," *Parameters*, Vol. 39 (Spring 2009), 14.

14.   Amin Saikal, *Modern Afghanistan: A History of Struggle and Survival* (New York: I.B. Tauris, 2004), 7.

15.   Angelo Rasanayagam, *Afghanistan, A Modern History, 2nd ed.* (New York: I.B. Tauris, 2005), 184. The five autonomous Tribal Agencies that straddle the Durand line over which Pakistan technically has no jurisdiction.

16.   *Institute for the Study of War*, October 9, 2009. http://www.understandingwar.org/ afghanistan-project/maps (accessed 1 March 2010).

17.   *Institute for the Study of War.*

18.   Stephen Tanner, *Afghanistan: A Military History from Alexander the Great to the War Against the Taliban* (Philadelphia: Da Capo Press, 2002), 117-122.

19.   Louis Dupree, *Afghanistan, 3rd* ed. (Oxford: Oxford University Press, 1997), 335-339.

20.   Richard F. Nyrop and Donald M. Seekins, editors, *Afghanistan: A Country Study. 5th* ed. (Washington DC: US Government, 1986), 14-19.

21. Rasanayagam, *Afghanistan, A Modern History*, xiv, 1-3.

22. Saikal, *Modern Afghanistan*, 31-32.

23. Jalali, "Winning in Afghanistan," 76. "At the outbreak of the second Anglo-Afghan War (1878-80), the regular army was about 50,000 strong and consisted of 62 infantry and 16 cavalry regiments, with 324 guns mostly organized in horse and mountain artillery batteries. However, much of the organization existed only on paper. Poor training, lack of unit discipline, lack of unit cohesiveness, and inadequate officer education made the army a paper tiger."

24. Tanner, *Afghanistan: A Military History*, 202-207.

25. Rasanayagam, *Afghanistan, A Modern History*, xvi. The actual phrase "Great Game" was coined by a British Army officer Arthur Conolly, and made famous by Kipling.

26. Jalali, "Rebuilding Afghanistan's National Army," 72.

27. Jalali, 73.

28. Saikal, *Modern Afghanistan*, 35.

29. Tanner, *Afghanistan: A Military History*, 218.

30. Dupree, *Afghanistan*, 421.

31. Rasanayagam, *Afghanistan, A Modern History*, 2.

32. Saikal, *Modern Afghanistan*, 36.

33. Hafizullah Emadi, *Culture and Customs of Afghanistan* (Westport Connecticut: Greenwood Press, 2005), 7.

34. Rasanayagam, *Afghanistan, A Modern History*, 11.

35. Emadi, *Culture and Customs of Afghanistan*, 31.

36. Dupree, *Afghanistan*, 417.

37. Rasanayagam, *Afghanistan, A Modern History*, 9.

38. Dupree, *Afghanistan*, 418.

39. Tanner, *Afghanistan: A Military History*, 218.

40. Rasanayagam, *Afghanistan, A Modern History*, 12.

41. Jalali, "Rebuilding Afghanistan's National Army," 75.

42. Saikal, *Modern Afghanistan*, 37.

43. Emadi, *Culture and Customs of Afghanistan*, 31.

44. Dupree, *Afghanistan*, 428.

45. Saikal, *Modern Afghanistan*, 35.

46. Rasanayagam, *Afghanistan, A Modern History*, 11.

47. Rasanayagam, 12.

48. Jalali, "Rebuilding Afghanistan's National Army," 73.

49. Dupree, *Afghanistan*, 420.

50. Tanner, *Afghanistan: A Military History*, 219.

51. Emadi, *Culture and Customs of Afghanistan*, 32.

52. Saikal, *Modern Afghanistan*, 61.

53. Dupree, *Afghanistan*, 442.

54. Tanner, *Afghanistan: A Military History*, 219.

55. Emadi, *Culture and Customs of Afghanistan*, 31.

56. Tanner, *Afghanistan: A Military History*, 221.

57. Saikal, *Modern Afghanistan*, 64.

58. Tanner, *Afghanistan: A Military History*, 223.

59. Saikal, *Modern Afghanistan*, 65-69.

60. Dupree, *Afghanistan*, 448.

61. Saikal, *Modern Afghanistan*, 79.

62. Emadi, *Culture and Customs of Afghanistan*, 31.

63. Rasanayagam, *Afghanistan, A Modern History*, 20.

64. Rasanayagam, 21.

65. Rasanayagam.

66. Saikal, *Modern Afghanistan*, 72.

67. Tanner, *Afghanistan: A Military History*, 222.

68. Emadi, *Culture and Customs of Afghanistan*, 32-33.

69. Tanner, *Afghanistan: A Military History*, 218-219.

70. Rasanayagam, *Afghanistan, A Modern History*, 21.

71. Saikal, *Modern Afghanistan*, 77.

72. Saikal, 78.

73. Jalali, "Rebuilding Afghanistan's National Army," 77.

74. Saikal, *Modern Afghanistan*, 78.

75. Dupree, *Afghanistan*, 451.

76. Saikal, *Modern Afghanistan*, 74.

77. Dupree, *Afghanistan*, 452

78. Emadi, *Culture and Customs of Afghanistan*, 31.

79. Dupree, *Afghanistan*, 462. "My sons and successors should not try to introduce reforms of any kind in such a hurry as to set the people against their ruler, and they must bear in mind that in establishing a constitutional government, introducing more lenient laws, and modeling education upon the system of Western universities, they must adopt all these gradually as people become accustomed to the idea of modern innovations."

80. Rasanayagam, *Afghanistan, A Modern History*, 21.

81. Dupree, *Afghanistan*, 450. "Rumors flew that the kingdom planned to bring back from Europe machines to make soap out of corpses. The King . . . had turned against Allah and Islam!"

82. Emadi, *Culture and Customs of Afghanistan*, 33. "Sadiq Mojaddadi collected signatures of 400 clerics who issued a religious decree (fatwa) condemning the King for violating Islamic values and pronouncing him unfit to rule."

83. Jalali, "Rebuilding Afghanistan's National Army," 77.

84. Saikal, *Modern Afghanistan*, 107.

85. Rasanayagam, *Afghanistan, A Modern History*, 23.

86. Dupree, *Afghanistan*, 464. "Collection of extracts from the Turkish, Iranian, and French constitutions as well as the 1923 Constitution, plus many aspects of the Hyundai fee Shari'a of Sunni Islam, and local custom ('*adat*)."

87. M. Nazif Shahrani, "State Building and Social Fragmentation In Afghanistan," *The State, Religion and Ethnic Politics: Afghanistan, Iran, and Pakistan*, ed. Ali Banuazizi and Myron Weiner (Syracuse, NY: Syracuse University Press, 1986). "To rule according to the Shariat of Mohammed . . . and the fundamental rules of the country and to strive for the protection of the glorious religion of Islam, the independence of Afghanistan and the rights of the nation, and for the defense, progress and prosperity of the country."

88. Saikal, *Modern Afghanistan*, 99.

89. Dupree, *Afghanistan*, 463.

90. Saikal, *Modern Afghanistan*, 102. Nadir's foreign policy was "positive neutrality and reciprocal friendship" with all states and sought to achieve two immediate objectives: non-provocative balanced relationships with both Great Britain and the Soviet Union, and acceptance by Muslim states.

91. Saikal, 99.

92. Jalali, "Rebuilding Afghanistan's National Army," 77.

93. Jalali, 77. Katawz rebellion in 1937-39; Shinwari revolt of 1938; Alizai-Durani unrest in 1939; 1944-45 rebellion of the Safi tribe in eastern Kunar province.

94. Rasanayagam, *Afghanistan, A Modern History*, 23.

95. Emadi, *Culture and Customs of Afghanistan*, 35.

96. Emadi, 34. May 1930 Shinwari tribes led rebellion in favor of Amanullah, Ghilzai tribe uprising southwest region of Kabul, Kohistan rebellion July 1930 brutally crushed with Pashtun militia.

97. Emadi, 35. Sayed Kamal assassinated Nadir's brother Mohammad Aziz, German Ambassador; Abdul Khaliq, a Hazara student at Nijat High School, assassinated Nadir during a student award presentation.

98. SAMS Seminar 9, Class 09-02. *From The "Village" to a Nation; The Narrative of Afghanistan in 2009.* (CGSC, Fort Leavenworth, Kansas: 15 October 2009), 2.

99. Jalali, "Rebuilding Afghanistan's National Army," 79.

100. Rasanayagam, *Afghanistan, A Modern History*, 259.

101. Saikal, *Modern Afghanistan*, 237.

102. Jalali, "Winning in Afghanistan," 8.

103. General Stanley McChrystal. ISAF Commander's Counterinsurgency Guidance,

August 2009, ISAF Headquarters,http://www.nato.int/isaf/docu/official_texts/counterinsurgency_ guidance.pdf (accessed 1 October 2009), 1. "We will not win simply by killing insurgents. We will help the Afghan people win by securing them, by protecting them from intimidation, violence, and abuse, and by operating in a way that respects their religion and culture. This means that we must change the way that we think, act, and operate. We must get people involved in the active success of their communities."

104. Curt Tarnoff, "Afghanistan: US Foreign Assistance," Congressional Research Service, (14 July 2009), http://www.fas.org/sgp/crs/row/R40699.pdf (accessed 1 October 2009), 3. 14 NATO countries lead the 26 Provincial Reconstruction Teams (PRTs) located in the majority of Afghan provinces. The United States leads 12 of these. The US PRTs are funded under two main programs to meet their objectives - DOD's Commander's Emergency Response Program (CERP), and USAID's Local Governance and Community Development Program.

105. Katzman, "Afghanistan: Post-Taliban Governance, Security, and US Policy," 45. There has long been consideration to turn over the lead in the US-run PRTs to civilians rather than military personnel, presumably State Department or USAID officials. As of November 2009, the "civilianization" of the PRT concept has evolved further with the decision to refer to PRTs as Interagency Provincial Affairs (IPA) offices or branches. In this new concept, higher level State Department officers will enjoy enhanced decision making status at each PRT, in concert with rather than subordinate to a military officer who commands the PRT.

106. Charles H. Briscoe, et al., *Weapon of Choice: ARSOF in Afghanistan* (Leavenworth, Kansas, Combat Studies Institute Press, 2004), 347.

107. Jalali, "Rebuilding Afghanistan's National Army," 72.

108. Lieutenant Colonel David Hylton, "100 Days of NTM-A," http://www.ntm-a.com/ news/1-categorynews/194-100-days-ofntm-a (accessed 1 March 2010).

109. Video Teleconference (VTC) with LTG William B. Caldwell, IV, CG, and select staff, NTM-A, Marshall Hall, CGSC, Fort Leavenworth, Kansas, February 11, 2010, 0730 (CST).

110. "ISAF and ANA Strength and Laydown," 1 October 2009, http://www.nato.int/isaf/docu/ epub/pdf/placemat.pdf (accessed 16 April 2010).

111. "ISAF and ANA Strength and Laydown".

112. *Institute for the Study of War*, October 9, 2009. http://www.understandingwar.org/ afghanistan-project/maps (accessed 1 March 2010).

113. *Institute for the Study of War*.

114. SAMS Seminar 9, *From the "Village" to a Nation*, 7.

115. Tarnoff, "Afghanistan: US Foreign Assistance," 1. The FY2010 budget request to Congress would provide $2.8 billion in economic assistance under the State Department, $7.5 billion for Afghan Security Forces and $1.5 billion for CERP (shared with Iraq) under the Defense Department.

116. Kenneth Katzman, "Afghanistan: Post-Taliban Governance, Security, and US Policy," 4. 40% unemployment rate; 80% of the population is involved in agriculture. Self-sufficiency in wheat production as of May 2009 (first time in 30 years). Products for export include fruits, raisins, melons, pomegranate juice ("*anar*"), nuts, carpets, lapis lazuli gems, marble tile, timber

products (Kunar, Nuristan provinces). In 2009, large exports of pomegranates and apples to India and Dubai began.

117. Tarnoff, "Afghanistan: US Foreign Assistance," 7. CERP performs a development function often indistinguishable from the activities of USAID and is a major tool of US PRTs. Mostly used for infrastructure – 66% used for road repair and construction.

118. Michael Moore and James Fussell, "Kunar and Nuristan, Rethinking US Counterinsurgency Operations," *Afghanistan Report 1*, (Washington DC: Institute for the Study of War, 2009), 25. "These smaller projects often times better demonstrate the benefit of an expanded American presence in Afghan villages. US forces must assess the needs of the local populations and give them immediate, quantifiable humanitarian assistance such as medical and dental aid, radios, and blankets. Not only will this support and demonstrate that the population is the center of gravity, but it will raise the cost of infiltration for the insurgents."

119. MG Michael T. Flynn and Captain Matt Pottinger, "Fixing Intel: A Blueprint for Making Intelligence Relevant in Afghanistan," *Voices From The Front* (Center For A New American Security, 2010), 1.

120. Flynn and Pottinger, "Fixing Intel," 21. Community information centers being set up at regional commands that provide on classified versions intelligent assessments providing access to all. The efforts are supported by Lieutenant General Rodriguez and General McChrystal. Information includes white intelligence as well as host nation information.

121. Lieutenant General David M. Rodriguez, Commander of the ISAF Joint Command. "Supporting the Afghan Environment," The Afghan Hands Blog. http://www.isaf.nato.int/en/the-afghan-hands-blog/commanders-blog/supporting-the-afghan-environment-david-m.-rodriquez-ijc-commander.html (accessed 1 April 2010). "Understanding the complexity of the Afghan people, then, requires a great depth of understanding of information, not just intelligence, about the Afghan people. We depend on good information and an understanding of the people if we hope to succeed, to help the Afghans build tailored solution sets that respond to the needs of their people."

122. Nyrop and Seekins, *Afghanistan: A Country Study*, 13-14.

123. Rasanayagam, *Afghanistan, A Modern History*, xvi.

124. Michael Miklaucic, "The Tea Fallacy," *Small Wars Journal*, http://smallwarsjournal.com/blog/journal/docs-temp/391-miklaucic.pdf (accessed 1 March 2010).

Bibliography

Blood, Peter R., ed. "Afghanistan: A Country Study." *Library of Congress -- Federal Research Division.* http://purl.access.gpo.gov/GPO/LPS39921 (accessed December 1, 2009).

Bauman, Robert F. *Russian-Soviet Unconventional Wars in the Caucasus, Central Asia, and Afghanistan.* Leavenworth Paper Number 20. Fort Leavenworth, Kansas: Combat Studies Institute, 1993.

Bowman, Steve and Catherine Dale. "War in Afghanistan: Strategy, Military Operations, and Issues for Congress." *Congressional Research Service.* February 25, 2010. http://www.fas.org/sgp/crs/natsec/R40156.pdf (accessed March 1, 2010).

—. "War in Afghanistan: Strategy, Military Operations, and Issues for Congress." *Congressional Research Service.* February 25, 2010. http://www.fas.org/sgp/crs/natsec/ R40156.pdf (accessed March 1, 2010).

Briscoe, Charles H., Richard L. Kiper, James A. Schroder, and Kalev I. Sepp. *Weapon of Choice: ARSOF in Afghanistan.* Leavenworth, Kansas: Combat Studies Institute Press, 2004.

Caldwell, LTG William B., IV, CG and select staff, NTM-A. "Video Teleconference." Fort Leavenworth, Kansas: Marshall Hall, CGSC, 0730 (CST), February 11, 2010.

CIA - The World Fact Book. October 5, 2009. https://www.cia.gov/library/ publications/the-world-factbook/geos/af.html (accessed March 1, 2010).

"Country Profile: Afghanistan." *Library of Congress -- Federal Research Division.* August 2008. http://lcweb2.loc.gov/frd/cs/profiles/Afghanistan.pdf (accessed October 1, 2009).

Dupree, Louis. *Afghanistan.* Oxford: Oxford University Press, 1997.

Emadi, Hafizullah. *Culture and Customs of Afghanistan.* Westport, Connecticut: Greenwood Press, 2005.

Facts and Figures: Afghan National Army. NATO Factsheet, Media Operations Centre, Brussels, Belgium: NATO Headquarters, December 2009.

Flynn, MG Michael T., Captain Matt Pottinger and Paul D. Batchelor. *Fixing Intel: A Blueprint for Making Intelligence Relevant in Afghanistan.* Working Papers, Voices from the Front, Center for a New American Security, 2010.

Goodson, Larry. *Afghanistan's Endless War: State Failure, Regional Politics, and the Rise of the Taliban.* Seattle, Washington: University of Washington Press, 2001.

Grau, Lester W. *The Bear Went Over the Mountain: Soviet Combat Tactics in Afghanistan.* 10th Edition. Washington, DC: National Defense University Press Publications, 2005.

—. *The Soviet-Afghan War: How a Superpower Fought and Lost.* Lawrence, Kansas: Kansas University Press, 2001.

Hendrickson, D. and A.Karkoszka. "The Challenges of Security Sector Reform." In *SIPRI Yearbook 2002: Armaments, Disarmament and International Security*, 175 - 201. Oxford: Oxford University Press, 2002.

Howk, Jason C. "A Case Study in Security Sector Reform: Learning from Security Sector Reform / Building in Afghanistan (October 2002-September 2003)." *Peace Keeping and Stability Operations Institute, Strategic Studies Institute*. USAWC. November 2009. http://www.strategicstudiesinstitute.army.mil/pubs/display. cfm?pubID=949 (accessed December 1, 2009).

Hylton, Lieutenant Colonel David. *100 Days of NTM-A*. 2010. http://www.ntm-a. com/news/1-categorynews/194-100-days-ofntm-a (accessed March 1, 2010).

Institute for the Study of War. October 9, 2009. http://www.understandingwar.org/ afghanistan-project/maps (accessed March 1, 2010).

ISAF and ANA Strength and Laydown. October 1, 2009. http://www.nato.int/isaf/ docu/epub/pdf/placemat.pdf (accessed March 1, 2010).

Jalali, Ali A. and Lester W. Grau. *The Other Side of the Mountain: Mujahideen Tactics in the Soviet-Afghan War*. Quantico, Virginia: USMC Studies and Analysis Division, 1995.

Jalali, Ali A. "Rebuilding Afghanistan's National Army." *Parameters, USAWC Quarterly*, Autumn 2002.

Jalali, Ali A. "Winning in Afghanistan." *Parameters, USAWC Quarterly*, Spring 2009.

Jalili, Ali A. *Clashes of Ideas and Interests in Afghanistan*. Washington, DC: Institute of World Politics, 1995.

Jones, General James L. USMC (ret) and Ambassador Thomas R. Pickering. *Afghanistan Study Group Report: Revitalizing Our Efforts, Rethinking Our Strategies*. Washington, DC: Center for the Study of the Presidency, January 30, 2008, 2nd Edition.

Kagan, Kimberly. "Afghan Army and Police Forces Must Grow Much Larger." *Washington Examiner*, August 18, 2009.

Katzman, Kenneth. "Afghanistan: Post-Taliban Governance, Security, and US Policy." *Congressional Research Service*. March 1, 2010. http://www.fas.org/sgp/crs/row/ RL30588.pdf (accessed March 1, 2010).

Lubold, Gordon. "Americans Build Elite Afghan Commando Force." *Christian Science Monitor*, May 1, 2008.

McChrystal, General Stanley A. "Commander's Initial Assessment." *Washington Post*. August 30, 2009. http://media.washingtonpost.com/wp-srv/politics/ (accessed March 1, 2010).

—. "ISAF Commander's Counterinsurgency Guidance." International Security Assistance Force Headquarters. August 2009. http://www.nato.int/isaf/docu/official_texts/ counterinsurgency_guidance.pdf (accessed October 1, 2009).

McMichael, Scott R. *Stumbling Bear: Soviet Military Performance in Afghanistan.* Brassey's (U.K.) Ltd., 1991.

Miklaucic, Michael. "The Tea Fallacy." *Small Wars Journal.* March 16, 2010. http://smallwarsjournal.com/blog/journal/docs-temp/391-miklaucic.pdf (accessed April 1, 2010).

"Military Specialists Aim to Improve Cultural Understanding." *ISAF Public Affairs Office.* U.K. Ministry of Defense. http://www.isaf.nato.int/en/article/news/military-specialists-aim-to-improve-cultural-understanding.html, (accessed April 1, 2010).

Moore, Michael and James Fussell. *Kunar and Nuristan: Rethinking US Counterinsurgency Operations.* Afghanistan Report I, Washington, DC: Institute for the Study of War, 2009, 25.

Morelli, Vincent and Paul Belkin. "NATO in Afghanistan: A Test of the Transatlantic Alliance." *Congressional Research Service.* December 3, 2009. http://www.fas.org/sgp/crs/row/RL33627.pdf (accessed March 1, 2010).

Naylor, Sean. *Not a Good Day to Die: The Untold Story of Operation Anaconda.* New York, NY: Berkley Books, 2004.

Nyrop, Richard F. and Donald M. Seekins, ed. *Afghanistan: A Country Study.* 5th Edition. Washington, DC: US Government, 1986.

Rasanayagam, Angelo. *Afghanistan, A Modern History.* New York: I.B. Tauris, 2005.

Rashid, Ahmed. *Jihad: The Rise of Militant Islam in Central Asia.* New Haven, Connecticut: Yale University Press, 2002.

—. *Taliban: Militant Islam, Oil and Fundamentalism in Central Asia.* New Haven, Connecticut: Yale University Press, 2001.

Rodriguez, Lieutenant General David M. *Supporting the Afghan Environment.* The Afghan Hands Blog. http://www.isaf.nato.int/en/the-afghan-hands-blog/commanders-blog/supporting-the-afghan-environment-david-m.-rodriquez-ijc-commander.html (accessed April 1, 2010).

Saikal, Amin. *Modern Afghanistan; A History of Struggle and Survival.* New York: I.B. Tauris, 2004.

SAMS Seminar 9, Class 09-02. "From the "Village" to a Nation: The Narrative of Afghanistan in 2009." *CGSC, Fort Leavenworth, Kansas*, October 2009.

Shahrani, M. Nazif. "State Building and Social Fragmentation in Afghanistan." In *The State, Religion, and Ethnic Politics: Afghanistan, Iran, and Pakistan*, edited by Ali Banuazizi and Myron Weiner. Syracuse, New York: Syracuse University Press, 1986.

Stanton, Doug. *Horse Soldiers: The Extraordinary Story of a Band of US Soldiers Who Rode to Victory in Afghanistan.* New York, NY: Scribner, 2009.

Tamoff, Curt. "Afghanistan: US Foreign Assistance." *Congressional Research Service.* July 14, 2009. http://www.fas.org/sgp/crs/row/R40699.pdf (accessed October 1, 2009).

Tanner, Stephen. *Afghanistan: A Military History From Alexander The Great To The War Against The Taliban.* Philadelphia, Pennsylvania: Da Capo Press, 2002.

Tariq, Mohammed Osman. *Tribal Secuirty System (Arbakai) in Southeast Afghanistan.* Occasional Paper 7, Crisis States Research Centre, London: DESTIN, LSE, 2008.

TRADOC G2 Human Terrain System. *My Cousin's Enemy is My Friend: A Study of Pashtun "Tribes" in Afghanistan.* White Paper, United States Army, Fort Leavenworth, Kansas: Afghanistan Research Reachback Center, September 2009.

"White Paper of the Interagency Policy Group's Report on US Policy Toward Afghanistan and Pakistan." *Interagency Policy Group.* Office of the President, Washington, DC March 2009. http://www.whitehouse.gov/assets/documents/Afghanistan-Pakistan_White_Paper.pdf (accessed March 2, 2010).

Yousaf, Mohammad and Mark Adkin. *The Bear Trap: Afghanistan's Untold Story.* London: Leo Cooper, 1992.

Algerian Perspectives of Counterinsurgencies

Major Jose R. Laguna

Recent scholarly work has devoted much attention to analyzing the French counterinsurgency war in Algeria from 1954 to 1962. The United States military has taken many of the lessons and principles offered by authors such as David Galula and Roger Trinquier based on this conflict and placed them into its doctrine. This monograph serves to explore other examples of internal conflicts in Algeria in light of the popular model normally presented by the insurgency against French occupation in 1954. It proposes that population centric counterinsurgency emphasizes a direct approach to the population. It will show that in two other instances in Algeria an indirect model of counterinsurgency proved more effective. The study will commence with a brief review of the 1954-1962 war of independence from France and the counterinsurgency theory that emerged from it. Next, the study explores the Ottoman experience in Algeria from 1515 to 1830. Subsequently, the work will review the recent Algerian Civil War (1991-2002). The monograph will conclude with an analysis of the applicability of current counterinsurgency doctrine, as derived from the French theory, to the other insurgencies in Algeria. It will further show that the US chose as a model a theory that proved strategically ineffective in Algeria.

Introduction

In a recent article published by the United States Army War College, Colonel Gian Gentile notes, "Population-centric counterinsurgency (COIN) has become the American Army's new way of war."[1]

He argues that the United States Army has taken an "ahistorical" approach focusing on a narrow set of lessons "learned while combating the FLN insurgents in Algeria, Malaya Communist insurgents, and other Communist-inspired insurgencies."[2] Indeed, recent scholarly work has devoted a lot of attention analyzing the French counterinsurgency war in Algeria from 1954 to 1962. It provides a complex and large-scale example of a war of insurrection on the part of the Algerian nationalist of the National Liberation Front (FLN) against the French colonial government, which had been in existence since 1830. The United States military has taken many of the lessons and principles offered by authors such as David Galula and Roger Trinquier based on this conflict and placed them into its doctrine.[3] The most recent example is the Joint Publication 3-24: *Counterinsurgency Operations* released in October 2009.

This monograph serves to explore other examples of internal conflicts in Algeria in light of the popular model normally presented by the insurgency against French occupation in 1954. It proposes that population centric counterinsurgency emphasizes a direct approach to the population. It will show that in two other instances in Algeria an indirect model of counterinsurgency proved more effective.

The conflict of 1954-62 ended the French colonial rule in Algeria, but there were other counterinsurgencies, both before and after, which took place in Algeria. Prior to the French invasion of 1830, the Ottoman Empire ruled a population of millions with a small and ethnically distinct military caste in a state of constant conflict for the better part of three centuries. Persistent and costly struggles between the Turkish rulers and indigenous tribes led the Ottomans to adopt policies of ever-increasing autonomy for the Algerians under a Regency system.[4] The Ottomans focused their efforts on controlling the elites, protecting their strategic interests, and manipulating internal rivalries to achieve control.

In 1991, Islamists in Algeria began to make gains on establishing political strongholds with the population of Algeria. That year the government, still under the control of the non-secular FLN, cancelled elections in fear that the Islamic Salvation Front (FIS) could win the elections. Following this decision, the military took control of the government and forced the President Chadli Bendjedid to resign. The military led government then banned FIS and had several members arrested in an effort to consolidate control. Subsequently several Islamist armed groups emerged and began to conduct violent campaigns against the government and the people of Algeria. The conflict ran a complex and bloody course until 2002 when the Algerian government attained the surrender of two of the largest armed groups, the Islamic Salvation Army and the Armed Islamic Group. Estimates show that the conflict cost between 150,000 and 200,000 lives.[5]

The study will commence with a brief review of the 1954-1962 war of independence from France and the counterinsurgency theory that emerged from it. Next, the study explores the Ottoman experience in Algeria from 1515 to 1830. Subsequently, the work will review the recent Algerian Civil War (1991-2002). The monograph will conclude with an analysis of the applicability of current counterinsurgency doctrine, as derived from the French theory, to the other insurgencies in Algeria.

The study will show that, in Algeria, the population centric approach proved the least strategically feasible and ultimately unsuccessful. Both the Ottomans and the Algerians applied a more indirect approach towards the population and were more successful than the French were in protecting their strategic interests from internal threats. Based solely on the experiences in Algeria, it would appear that the US highlighted a theory of counterinsurgency which is costly and strategically ineffective.

Setif, War of Independence 1954-1962, and the emergence of Counterinsurgency Theory

The nationalist sentiment that gained popularity under Abdelhanid Ben Badis and the Association of Muslim Algeria Ulema, and Messali Hadj and the *Etoile Nord-Africaine* (ENA) in the 1930s rekindled on May 8, 1945 (VE Day). There had been a few indicators of mounting hostilities against the colons in the form of rock throwing incidents, graffiti, and minor civil disobedience in the weeks prior to that Tuesday. The French authorities had received information that an insurrection was brewing and had issued orders banning the display of inflammatory material. That morning, thousands of Muslim Algerians demonstrated in city streets across Algeria displaying green and white flags signifying the standard of the resistance against the French employed by Abd-el-Kader in the 1840s. The demonstrations were organized by members of numerous political parties that ran from the more nationalist PPA (who had been outlawed) to the more moderate *Amis du Manifeste et de la Liberte (AML)* under the leadership of Ferhat Abbas and with some degree of approval given by Messali Hadj.[6] The demonstrations would coincide with the celebration of the victory in Europe. Most of the demonstrations went off without the emergence of violence, although most met some degree of antagonism on the part of the *colons*.[7] Setif, however, sparked five days of chaotic violence with an estimated 6,000 Algerians and 103 Europeans killed.

Setif is a small mining and farm town 80 miles west of Constantine and, unlike the larger cities of Oran and Algiers, was predominantly Muslim with a history of nationalist fervor. Poor crops during the previous two years had devastating effects on the population of Algeria. Though food was not as scarce around Setif as in other areas, the presence of large European owned farms that were prospering from preferential treatment proved insidious to the Muslim population. Amplifying this effect was the fact that Vichy France depleted rations stored in Algeria for use in supporting the war effort of Germany.[8] May 8, 1945 also coincided with market day in Setif, which brought farmers and merchants from the neighboring countryside into the town. An estimated crowd of 8,000 Algerians gathered to protest carrying banners and flags. The twenty police in the town encountered the demonstrators and altercations broke out leading to gun fire.[9] The demonstrators countered by attacking police and Europeans, which began a spontaneous cycle of reciprocating violence. Violence quickly spread to the countryside between the towns of Setif and Guelma and the mountains of Kabyle, surrounding Constantine.

In response, the French deployed 10,000 troops into the area and began a *ratissage* operation (literally raking over) to repress the Algerian militants.[10] During the week following the initiation of military operations, the French Army showed little restrain in putting down the insurrection. The operations included the use of Senegalese ground units, Aerial bombardment and strafing, and even Naval Artillery on Arab and Kabyle villages. Accounts point to numerous instances of indiscriminate use of force and summary executions on the part of the French forces. Additionally the violence on both Algerian and European sides were unusually brutal and included violence against children, rapes, and mutilations.[11] After a week, the majority of the insurrection was under control, though clean-up operations lasted through the end of May. Arrests by the French authorities continued throughout that year with 5,560 Muslims imprisoned and 99 sentenced to death.[12] The Governor General of Algeria arrested Ferhat Abbas, who had been a moderate and condemned the violence during the ordeal.

The Setif incident and the reprisals following marked a turning point for the nationalist movement in Algeria. Shortly after Setif, thousands of young Algerian men returned home from wartime service to France. Many of these soldiers came from Constantine and the surrounding areas where the some of the most violent actions occurred. Some of the future members and leaders of the FLN were among those soldiers. France largely overlooked the effects that this had on Algeria predominately due to their occupation with domestic issues of the metropolitan, which were plentiful in the days following liberation. In France, the popular belief was that the incidents nothing more than food riots and not a true call for independence. The belief was still strong that there was no existence of an Algerian identity separate from a French colony. This sentiment prevailed despite the warnings from the military commander responsible for the pacification of the riots who stated, "I have given you peace for ten years but don't deceive yourselves...."[13] The colons were shocked at the violence and fearful that it would be repeated in the future and demanded more oppressive measures and the suspension of reforms. The result of Setif was further polarization of the communities in Algeria.[14]

The French military's response reflects their recent experience in World War II. The response was limited in time and geography to the source of the belligerents and executed with models developed by Nazi-Germany and Vichy France for anti-partisan operations in occupied territories. In essence, it reflected the conventional response of the time.

The Algerian war for independence began in 1954 and ended in 1962 when French President Charles De Gaulle pronounced Algeria an independent country on July 3. The war played out in three distinct phases; the birth of the FLN and associated popular movements and the FLN's consolidation of power (1954-1957), the Open War of French military victories and political defeats (1957-1959), and the bloody search for a political end (1960-62).

From this experience in Algeria, and those in Indochina, the French developed a theory of counterinsurgency that had a profound influence on the US Army's contemporary counterinsurgency doctrine. The works of Roger Trinquier, *Modern Warfare: A French View of Counterinsurgency,* and David Galula, *Counter-Insurgency Warfare: Theory and Practice,* define the American interpretation of the lessons and doctrines employed and recommended by the French Army of the time. The authors approach their study by examining how the goals and techniques of anti-colonial and communist insurgents differed from traditional warfare. They conclude that traditional methods focused on the defeat of an enemy in battle would not work in counterinsurgencies because the insurgent's military arm is too elusive and even when defeated, the insurgency will continue because it feeds off a vast clandestine organization. [15] The authors each assert that the key to winning the insurgency is winning the battle for the population. In essence, the population is the insurgent's center of gravity. Trinquier offers three principles that drive operations in counterinsurgencies, "to cut the guerrilla off from the population that sustains him; to render guerrilla zones untenable; and to coordinate these actions over a wide area and for long enough, so that these steps will yield the desired results."[16] David Galula offers four laws for counterinsurgency. The first law states, "The support of the population is as necessary to the counterinsurgent as for the insurgent."[17] Again, this law makes the population the objective and the source of strength for both the insurgent and the counterinsurgent. The second law is that "Support is gained through an active minority."[18] This law states that the population generally falls into three categories consisting of a minority who actively supports the insurgent, an active minority who supports the counterinsurgent, and a neutral majority. The problem then becomes how to boost the active minority who supports the counterinsurgent and mobilize the neutral majority against the insurgent minority. The third law states "Support from the population is conditional."[19] In order to receive support, the population must believe that the counterinsurgent has the will, means, and ability to win and that it can safeguard them from the insurgent's violence. The fourth law follows from the third law in stating, "Intensity of efforts and vastness of means are essential."[20] This law speaks to the necessity to commit large concentration of efforts in personnel and resources for a long duration in order to win over the confidence of the population.

In the early morning hours of November 1, 1954, Algeria erupted into explosions. Egyptian radio announcements explained that the coordinated attacks on police stations, barracks, and industrial plants throughout the cities signaled the start of the Algerian war of Independence. The date coincided with the catholic holiday of All Saints' Day. The *Front de Liberation Nationale* (FLN) leadership chose a day that afforded reduced police vigilance, and maximum propaganda value.[21] The FLN marked the birth of their movement with a grand proclamation that communicated a vision of an independent social democratic nation within an Islamic framework.[22]

The French response was immediate. Within hours, France mobilized 600 French police and flew them into Algeria by that afternoon. The French Prime Minister, Pierre Medes-France, quickly established a policy that separated Algeria from other colonies such as Vietnam and Tunisia. In a speech delivered on 12 November 1954, Mendes-France set the communicated the policy to the French National Assembly, "One does not compromise when it comes to defending the internal peace of the nation, the unity and the integrity of the Republic...*Mesdames, Messieurs*, several deputies have made comparisons between French policy in Algeria and Tunisia. I declare that no parallel is more erroneous, that no comparison is falser, or more dangerous. *Ici, c'est la France!*[Here it is France]."[23]

The FLN had hoped that the All Saints' Day attacks would galvanize Algerian independence emotions and cause the French Government to reappraise its policy. However, the offensive failed to meet the scope and expectations its initiators. Within two weeks police dismantled the insurgent network in Algiers acting on intelligence provided by local informants. On January 15, 1955 the French troops killed the leader of the FLN in Constantinois, Didouche Mourad, in a small skirmish in Constantine. On January 20, 1955 the French army launched a major operation in the Aures. In the mountains, the French mechanized force deployed to put down the unrest proved ill equipped for the operations lacking the mobility, training, and intelligence support from *pied noirs* required to pursue the insurgents.[24]

The lessons from these operations, along with the French experiences in Indochina, began to form the French theory of counterinsurgency.[25] They recognized the inadequacies of traditional warfare and the need to combine police action with military action to be effective in counterinsurgency. Roger Trinquier, in *Modern Warfare: A French View of Counterinsurgency*, asserts that "Police action will therefore be actual operational warfare. It will be methodically pursued until the enemy organization has been entirely annihilated."[26] He further discounts the use of large unit sweeps of short duration that "temporarily disperse guerrilla bands rather than destroy them."[27] The principle purpose of police operations should, in his view, be to gather the intelligence necessary not just to neutralize the insurgent, but to dismantle the entire organization "that feeds him, informs him, and sustains his morale."[28]

In the months preceding the inaugural offensive, six educated rebel leaders (Ben Boulaid, Larbi Ben M'hidi, Didouche Mourad, Rabah Bitah, Krim Belkacern, and Mohammed Boudiaf) created the Revolutionary Committee of Unity and Action (CRUA).[29] It succeeded in establishing an internal organization and vision that provided the structure for the next seven and a half years of insurrection. It divided the country into five (an additional sixth was later added) military districts known as *wilayas*. Each district further divided into zones (*mantaqa*s), regions (*nahayas*), sectors (*qasmas*), and finally circles (*duwwars*).[30] The districts were to have a leader (colonel) with an assistant for political affairs, one for logistics, and one for information. The further subdivisions were to have lesser officers and NCOs with assistant to provide the same basic functions (logistics, political affairs, information). The military arm had not yet developed fully in 1954, but consisted of loose organizations comprised of regulars (called *moujahidines* or *fellaghas*) and auxiliaries (called *mousseblines*). Later, regular forces organized into the *Armee de Leberation Nationale*, or ALN. Ideally, a commander of regulars (*moujahidines*) worked in a number of subdivisions (sectors), and the regional commanders were responsible for providing auxiliary forces, however, this was not always the case in reality. The subdivision commanders were responsible for providing intelligence, support and counterintelligence to the regulars and for mobilizing popular support.[31]

Realizing they had failed to gain the support of the Muslim population to join the rebellion, the FLN leaders opted to raise the level of violence to incite hatred and fear among the population. On 20 August, 1955, Zighoud Youcef, Mourad's successor, launched a series of operations in north Constantinois centered on the cities of Collo, Philippeville, Constantine, and Guelma. A few uniformed regulars from the *Armee de Liberation Nationale* (ALN, the armed branch of the FLN) organized and led the attacks. For the first time the FLN openly lifted restrictions on women and children and authorized the execution of Muslim political elite. When French troops arrived at a village near Philippeville (El-Halia), "an appalling sight greeted them. In houses literally awash with blood, European mother were found with their throats slit and their bellies slashed open with bill-hooks. Children had suffered the same fate, and infants in arms had their brains dashed out against the wall."[32]

As terrorism emerged as a tactic in Algeria, the French began to study it and to analyze how insurgents used it to further their cause. David Galula offers two types of terrorism; blind terrorism and selective terrorism. Blind terrorism consists of random spectacular acts perpetrated to gain attention to the insurgents cause and to attract "latent supporter."[33] Selective terrorism aims at isolating the counterinsurgent from the population and consists for assassinations of key individuals who work closely with the population.[34]

In February 1956, newly elected French Prime Minister Guy Mollet installed a hard liner politician, Robert Lacoste as governor general of Algeria. Under Mollet, the French government established their policy towards Algeria. This policy sought to win the war first, and then establish moderate reforms to appease the Algerian elites, while maintaining *pieds noirs* as the ruling caste and quelling the international pressure for decolonization.[35] In order to win the war first, the military strategy sought to increase the number of forces dramatically and conduct a population focused counterinsurgency campaign. In March and April 1956, the French government authorized exceptional measures and special powers to suppress violence in Algeria. Algeria was divided into three zones; a zone of operation where the objective was to crush the rebels, a zone of pacification which sought to protect Europeans and friendly Muslims, and a forbidden zone where whole populations were resettled into camps and placed under the control of the army. French authorities began to conduct mass arrests, detentions, and interrogations.[36] In November 1956, the French government appointed General Raoul Salan, a veteran of the Indochina counterinsurgency, as the commander of the armed forces in Algeria.[37] The French increased their army in Algeria to 400,000 by 1956.

The French approach, described by Galula and Trinquier, calls for a methodical system of dividing the territories (*quadrillage*) in to categorized zones according to level of security (white area-secured, red areas-insurgent strongholds, pink areas-contested territory).[38] Then operations focus on clearing a designated area of insurgents, building a secure environment that the counterinsurgent can control, and then spreading out from that secured area to roll back the territory and support available to the insurgent. This system, often referred to as *inkspot,* is the foundation for what US Army Field Manual 3-24: *Counterinsurgency* calls the Clear-Hold-Build approach.[39] This requires large amounts of troops in order to bring about the required level of security needed to uncover the organization that supports the insurgent.

In Algeria, the large-scale deployments initially resulted in further polarizing the population (*pied noirs* and Muslims) and driving more and more Muslims to side with the FLN.[40] The FLN began to receive the support they intended to incite in 1954. Faced with increasing escalation of French troops, and increasing alienation by the Colonial government, moderate Muslim elites (Ben Youssef Ben Khedda, Saad Dhalab, M'Hamed Yazid, and Hocine Lahouel- members of the UDMA) aligned themselves and their followers with the FLN. The number of members of the ALN began to swell, and by 1956, the FLN was leading a vast and complicated clandestine network that included guerilla forces, a diplomatic arm, political parties, and terrorist organizations.

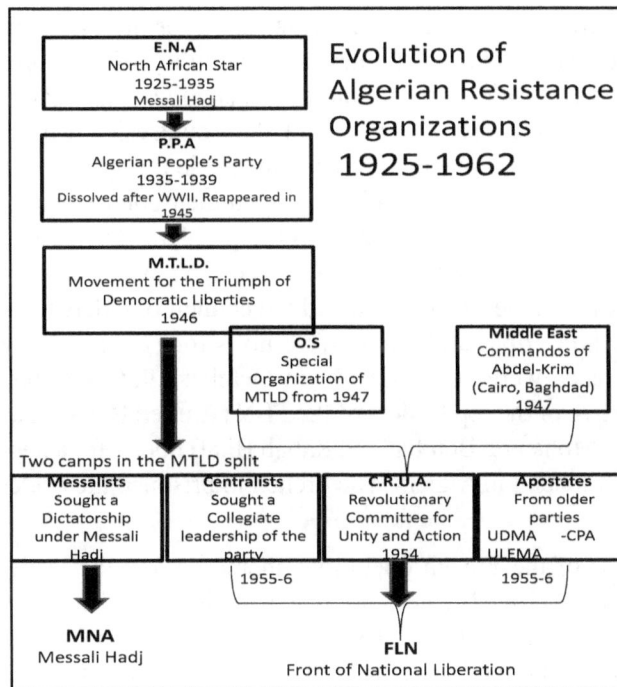

Evolution of Algerian resistance organizations, 1925-1962.

The challenge now for the FLN was to coordinate, assimilate, and co-opt all the different political and ideological interest of newly acquired supporters. The FLN provided a conduit for two major movements among the people of Algeria; the socialist movement and the traditional Islamic movement.[41] By the end of 1956, the FLN had only one remaining political challenger, the M.N.A. of Messali Hadj, and it only seriously influenced the Algerian Diaspora.[42]

The FLN understood victory through military means alone was not realistic, and gave great emphasis to exerting international political pressure on France. The diplomatic arm of the FLN composed of three offices; one in Cairo, one in New York, and one in Morocco. The efforts were led by Mohammed Khider working predominantly from Cairo, his brother-in-law (and former military leader of the MTLD) Hocine Ait Ahmed worked in New York and lobbied in the UN, and Ben Bella who travelled throughout the Middle East and Africa (office in Morocco). Their mission was to "defeat French efforts to define Algeria as an internal affair and to take the FLN's case to the United Nations."[43] Ben Bella also had the mission to acquire weapons, ammunitions, and supplies to feed the insurgency in Algeria.

On March 16, 1956, the FLN struck again with a wave of random killings in Algiers and Oran in retaliation of the new special powers legislation. In April 1956, Ferhat Abbas, a long time moderate nationalist officially joined the FLN. Additionally, both Tunisia and Morocco gained their independence in the spring of 1956 giving the insurgents safe staging grounds for their forces and equipment, "the new geographic reality greatly complicated France's pacification effort tactically and materially"[44]

The French tactics were increasingly devastating for the FLN command and control. The segregation of the *quadrillage* (zones) and the policy of *regroupement* (resettlement) effectively isolated the leadership and interdicted supplies and weapons, in effect "taking the water away from the fish."[45] Attacks in the countryside were progressively more difficult to orchestrate and movement restrictions made it impractical to surge the ALN to a location for action. The French greatly improved their counterinsurgency tactics as new and more experienced leaders weighed in on the problem. The new commanders studied local circumstances more closely and customized their operations to the environment.[46] For instance, in Kabylia the French co-opted the council of elders to extend control, while in Constantine (where tribal affiliations were not strong) zoning, psychological warfare and physical presence were emphasized.[47] In October 1956 the French interdicted a an airplane carrying five of the top leaders of the FLN (Ahmed Ben Bella, Hocine Ait Ahmed, Mohamed Khider, Mohamed Boudiaf and Rabah Bitat) bound for a negotiations meeting in Tunis and forced it to land in Algiers. The French imprisoned the leaders for the remainder of the war.[48]

As the success of the French operations increased and the leadership became more isolated, the FLN developed a new approach to the war. The architects of their new approach, Ramdane Abane and Ben M'Hidi, rationalized that operations in the countryside were becoming too costly and were insignificant to the international audiences. The new approach called for a focus on terrorism against the European populations of the cities.

On September 30, 1956, the FLN launched their campaign in Algiers under the direction of the Saadi Yacef, leader of the Algiers zone (nahaya). That day three young Muslim women, dressed to look like Europeans, planted bombs in heart of European Algiers in locations known to be favorite stops for families and young people returning from a day at the beach. Similar attacks followed into the winter of 1956. On December 28, the FLN assassinated the mayor of Algiers and followed up with a bomb at his funeral procession which targeted a crowed already "seething with anger."[49] In early January 1957, the FLN perpetrated another round of assassinations in the city.

Governor General Lacoste, facing challenges now from both the FLN and the *pieds noirs* escalated the conflict to an open war. On 7 January, Lacoste held a meeting with General Salan and General Jacques Massu, commander of the elite and renowned 10th Para Division. At the meeting, Lacoste granted Massu "full responsibility for maintenance of order in the city."[50] Through a combination of proven methods, Massu affected a stranglehold on the population of Algiers and the FLN networks. In early February, the FLN followed up with more bombings carried out by women in disguise, but by the end of the month, 10th Para had developed a more complete picture of Yacef's networks through its interrogation methods. Systematically, the FLN in Algiers began to crumble. The harsh tactics of the Army received widespread criticism in the media and in metropolitan France, but to the Army leaders the tactical success validated their approach. By the summer of 1957, Massu's forces had stopped a general strike, captured (later assassinated) Ben M'Hidi, the commander of district (wilaya) four, and forced the remaining leaders of the *Comite de Cordination et Execution* (CCE) to flee the country.[51]

During the same period, General Salan stepped up pressure against the ALN throughout the rest of the countryside. The French Army conducted major operations against Berber militias in the Grand Kabylia, and resettlement operations against rebel strongholds in villages north of Constantine. Meanwhile, the ALN had to fight battles against dissidents in the Aures who supported Messali Hadj and aligned with the French against the FLN.[52] The outlook for the FLN was bleak in 1957. More and more the insurgents had to rely on exterior lines of operations from Tunisia and Morocco. The French responded to this tactic by erecting the Morice line and other fortifications along the Tunisian and Moroccan borders, which it completed by the end of 1957.[53]

The French approach to counterinsurgency places great emphasis on the development of intelligence.[54] Both Galula and Trinquier assert that the key to gaining vital intelligence on the insurgents is creating a sense of safety in the population. By securing the population and giving them a stake in maintaining security, the counterinsurgent removes the barriers of intimidation protecting the clandestine organization. This, however, takes time to develop and much vital intelligence is lost. Trinquier, as with many French officers, endorsed the use of torture in order to gain time sensitive intelligence while Galula did not.[55] The use of torture and the strict measures imposed on the population, in order to create a secure environment, met with harsh criticism in France and in the international community.

In September 1957, the battle for Algiers ended with the capture of Saadi Yacef and the killing of his trusted lieutenant Ali la Pointe.[56] Dissention among the leader of the FLN emerged and in late 1957, FLN operatives assassinated Abane for supposedly attempting peace negotiations on his own. The remaining leaders of the FLN reorganized and reconstituted the CCE in Tunis in early 1958. Immediately, they came under bitter criticism for the decisions they had made. The criticism included the call for a general strike in the face of overwhelming French forces, the shift from the traditional rural strongholds into the weakly supported urban centers, and the move towards tactics that discredited the mujahidin by inciting repression.[57] Algiers was a costly loss of face for the FLN, particularly among the uncommitted Muslims of Algeria. After Algiers, the war shifted to the frontier where French might caused the resistance to stagnate.

For the French officers, the *pieds noirs*, and government officials in Algeria the successes were indisputable. For many officers and career soldiers of the French army, Algiers was a vindication and a bright victory in careers that had seen the fall of France in WWII, the bitter defeat of Dien Bien Phu, and the debacle of the Suez Canal in 1956.[58] The outlook was not the same in France. The commitment of nearly half a million soldiers to the war, many of them conscripts, meant a raising toll on the French youth. Many of the conscripts returned from the war with news and experiences that repulsed an already war weary population. The French government itself was turmoil stemming from bitter internal politics, mounting debts and a poor economy, and mounting international pressure.[59]

In February 1958, the French retaliated against ALN forces who had staged attacks from the Tunisian village of Sakiet by leveling the village with a squadron of American-built B-26 bombers. It was market day in Sakiet and hundreds of civilians packed the town. Newswires throughout the world carried the stories and photos depicting eighty Tunisian civilians killed and an addtional130 wounded.[60] The American and British governments now publicly announced their concern of the French handling of the war. In fact, Senator John F. Kennedy now became a vocal advocate for Algerian self-determination.[61] As it turned out, however, the army carried out the bombing without the approval of the French government.

Both Galula and Trinquier acknowledge the large role that international opinion played in Algeria and how the FLN used the actions of the counterinsurgent against them in propaganda. Trinquier even highlights the Tunisian bombardment to demonstrate the futility of traditional methods.[62] Their approach calls for extensive use of propaganda to target the population and the insurgents, but does not offer a means to address international audiences. Their efforts were proving effective at the tactical level, but were losing ground at the strategic level and losing the support of their countrymen.

On May 13, 1958, crowds of colons overthrew the government of Lacoste and installed the Committee of Public Safety, which included Generals Salan, Massu, Allard and Admiral Auboynau. From this platform, the Generals and opposition leaders in France (Gaullists) orchestrated the downfall of the Fourth Republic and reinstated Charles de Gaulle as the leader of the Fifth Republic.[63] With de Gaulle the Generals hoped to have a government that finally understood that the war in Algeria was about France, and that it required the will and commitment to win. For unknown reasons, the Generals chose to ignore de Gaulle's historical stance on Algeria and other colonies of France. As early as 1944, de Gaulle stated in a speech that it should be France's policy to "lead each of the colonial peoples to a development that will permit them to administer themselves, and later, to govern themselves."[64] As de Gaulle established his administration and restructured government under the Fifth Republic, further discussions and speeches on Algeria began to worry the *pieds noirs*. Weary of the climate of civil-military relationships, he purged some 1,500 officers from Algeria and recalled them back to France. Further, he ordered officers to withdraw from the Committee of Public safety, which subsequently disbanded. He promoted out General Salan and replaced him with an Air Force General, Maurice Challe.[65]

Meanwhile the FLN reorganized once again and formed the GPRA (Provisional Government of the Republic of Algeria). They also embarked on a new strategy to export the movement to metropolitan France and as the MNA (Messali Hadj) had done year prior. They intensified their recruitment efforts in France beginning in 1958 and by the next year doubled their membership 15,000, and to 150,000 by 1961. The support of the Diaspora generated large amounts of funding for the FLN and gave them a means to affect the French economy directly by orchestrating labor strikes.[66]

In 1959, de Gaulle escalated actions against the ALN in an effort to force the FLN into negotiations. That year General Challe conducted major operations in the districts of the Kabylia and Sahara (wilayas III and IV) which killed both of the FLN commanders. Under Challe's orders more than 2 million Algerians were displaced. In a stunning blow to many military leaders and the *pieds noirs,* de Gaulle announced his policy on Algeria on September 16, 1959 in a television address, "Given all the facts in Algeria, national and international, I consider it necessary that the recourse to self-determination be proclaimed beginning today."[67] In contrast to his military leaders, de Gaulle understood geopolitical reality of an international community committed to the decolonization movement and he decided that France's place was Europe, not Africa. The open war was over; all that remained was to find a political end.

Prime Minister de Gaulle replaced General Massu in January 1960, after criticizing the new policy in Algeria.[68] The *pieds noirs,* incensed with the turn on policy and the action of de Gaulle, formed their own rebellion. During "Barricades Week" the army that had defended Frenchmen from terrorists and guerillas for six years, was now defending itself from those same people based on a policy that most did not support. Militant *pieds noirs* staged insurrection that left fourteen dead and 123 wounded on January 24.[69]

The first round of talks between the FLN and the French government opened on June 25, 1960 and were a complete failure. The FLN position was that nothing short of complete self-determination was acceptable, French officials were not willing to accept. The FLN strategy was to increase international pressure within the UN and wait for France to further divide.[70] That year the FLN succeeded in rebuilding its networks in Algiers and in the suburbs. Despite the determination of de Gaulle to end the war in Algeria, the violence actually increased in 1960 as French army, the colons, and the Algerians all stepped up operations aimed at winning popular sentiment and separating each other from the population.

De Gaulle sought to cut the FLN out of the equation entirely and take a referendum directly to the people. In January 1961, the French president put forward a referendum concerning the establishment of public powers in Algeria under French supervision prior to self-determination (a transitional government). The referendum passed in both France and Algeria. As this was unfolding, the General Challe took an early retirement in protest. Later that same month Generals Salan, Jouhad, Zeller, and the newly retired Challe formed a clandestine organization called the Organisation Armee Secrete (OAS). Challe secretly flew back into Algiers and on 21 April 1961, using the parachute regiment of the Fist Foreign Legion initiated the "General's Putsch."[71] The OAS took over all key governmental and security facilities in Algiers that afternoon. The next morning Challe went on the radio and called for all the commanders to join the movement, which called for the takeover of the Republic and the reversal of policy on Algeria. Unfortunately, for the organizers, the remainder of the Army remained loyal to the government and on 25 April, Challe surrendered and the other officers were arrested or fled into hiding.[72] Thereafter, the OAS would operate secretively and proved to be a destructive force against movement toward self-determination.

The remainder of 1961 and into 1962 the OAS and FLN carried out a relentless campaign progressive retaliations. From January to February 1962 alone, there were 1,007 attacks in Algeria that caused 811 deaths and over 1500 wounded. In Paris region another 128 attacks occurred in the same time.[73] The official end of the war came with signing of the Evian accords on March 19, 1962, however, the violence continued well into the summer as the OAS became increasingly radical and the FLN began to punish the hariks (supporters of the French occupation).[74]

The dictums and principles developed by the French Army for counterinsurgency were sound and proved to have overwhelming effects against the FLN guerillas and terrorists working in the cities and hamlets of Algeria. The methodical process of their counterinsurgency eroded the insurgents' command and control, freedom of movement, and interdicted supplies to feed the insurgency. However, the level of commitment required in terms of lives and resources from the French citizenry, and the effect the tactics had on international and French public opinion proved too burdensome for France. In Algerian history, the Ottoman model of pacification provides a more pragmatic answer maintaining control of internal threats within the capacity of the government.

Pacification under Ottoman Rule

Algeria was the first territory in the Maghreb ruled by the Ottoman Empire. In 1515 Turkish privateering brothers, Aruj and Kahyr al-Din, were already operating in Tunisia. Algeria was divided by two weakening powers; in the east the sultanate of the Hafsids and in the west that of the Abd al Wadid dynasty. These powers were facing external threats from the Spanish and Hapsburgs who sought to establish bases along the Mediterranean coast. There was also increasing turmoil from tribal elites within the region (some of which had had arrangements with the Spanish). With the Spanish threat looming, elites from Algiers propositioned the al-Din brothers to help with the situation.[75] For the corsairs, establishing a base of operations in Algiers would allow the brothers to expand their privateering operations and divorce themselves from the Sultan of Tunis. On 1516, the brothers embarked on a campaign to wrest Algiers for themselves, which they accomplished in short term. Aruj would die in battle against a coalition of Spaniards and local tribes in Tlemcen in 1518. Kahyr al-Din, however, would prove to be tenacious and successful in dominating the area on both land and sea and earned the nickname Barbarossa from his European adversaries.[76] In 1519, Kahyr sought and received submission to the Ottoman government in exchange for reinforcements and material to continue his drive. The Sultan, Selim I, granted Khayr the royal title of Beylerbey (Governor General) of North Africa and with the title came the services of the Janissary infantry and artillery, and the full protection of the Ottoman Empire.[77] By 1529, he had driven the Spaniards and the Hafsids from Algiers, Penon, Tlemcen, and Constantine. By 1545 he had expelled the Abd al Wadids from western Algeria, defeated numerous Spanish attacks on the coastal cities, and defeated a naval invasion attempt by Charles V. Khayr would go on to become Admiral of the Ottoman Mediterranean fleet under the Sultan Suleiman I. His son Hasah Pasha took over after Kahyr retired in 1535 and would rule until 1552.

After 1552, the Ottoman government began assigning governors, called Pashas, over Algeria on fixed three-year rotations and did away with the office of beylerby in order to exert tighter control over the region. The structure excluded Arabs and Berbers from government posts and established Turkish as the official language. The actual effect of rotating Turkish rulers every three years meant that the Janissary officers, collectively known as the *ojaq*, exerted great power in the political institutions.[78] At its height in the early seventieth century, the Ottoman Empire maintained up to 15,000 Janissaries in Algiers.[79] The army in Algeria became increasingly powerful and harder to maintain. The pasha was responsible for paying the salaries of the army and the army itself controlled the government institutions.

The primary interest for the Ottoman rulers in Algeria was to control the Mediterranean, and privateering remained dominant source of revenue throughout its tenure. Therefore, the government and military served two purposes, to repel European expansion and to control the population in order to allow the corsairs to dominate the sea. On both of these fronts, the Turkish rulers of Algiers met numerous challenges throughout the seventeenth and eighteenth centuries. The Spanish occupied Tlemcen, bombarded Algiers, and held Oran from 1732 to 1792. The Kabyle tribes of the mountains of Grand Kabylia in northeast Algeira proved to be difficult to control and maintained a perpetual state of rebellion.

The topography in Algeria created an agricultural base that was limited and dispersed, making revenue difficult and dangerous to collect directly. Thus, corsair captains who comprised the *taifa al rais* controlled the primary source of funds to run the government and pay the Janissaries.[80] In the mid seventieth century, the *ojaq* staged numerous revolts against the pashas stemming from the inability of the pashas to pay their bimonthly salaries. At one point, they evicted the pasha and the commander of the Janissaries assumed rule, but the military leaders were no more successful in generating the necessary revenue. In 1671, the military finally turned to the *taifa al rais* and transferred supreme power to a corsair captain giving him the title of Dey and establishing a power sharing Regency between the dey and the pasha. Istanbul reluctantly accepted a new power-sharing concept, and the office of pasha became increasingly meaningless until 1710 when the dey assumed this title as well. A council of sixty representatives, known as the *divan*, selected the deys. This council was predominantly composed of Janissary officers, but later included larger participation by local religious and tribal elites. With this arrangement complete, "the Algerian elite had hit upon a formula which eventually permitted both stabilization of the political process and de facto independence of the Ottoman central government."[81]

The Ottomans exercised a loose but effective system of control over the population by segmenting tribes and religious groups and promoting competition amongst them, while ensuring the balance of power remained on the side of the Turkish elite. Additionally, throughout most of their tenure they demanded little in the form of taxation from majority of inhabitants.

By the seventeenth century, the Dey created three administrative territorial subdivisions know as *beyliks* (provinces), and in conjunction with the divan appointed Beys (governors) to administer and project power of the Regency. The Beylik of the East had its Capital in Constantine and was the largest and wealthiest due to a strong agricultural base and dominance over trade routes with Tunisia. In the center was the Beylik of Titteri, whose capital was Medea. The Western Beylik had its capital originally in Mascara and, upon expulsion of the Spanish, moved to Oran in 1794. The Western Beylik encompassed vast plains and valleys and a population dominated by nomads and semi nomads. Conflict was prevalent in the west due to enduring hostilities with Morocco and Spain and many tribes made a livelihood out of war.[82]

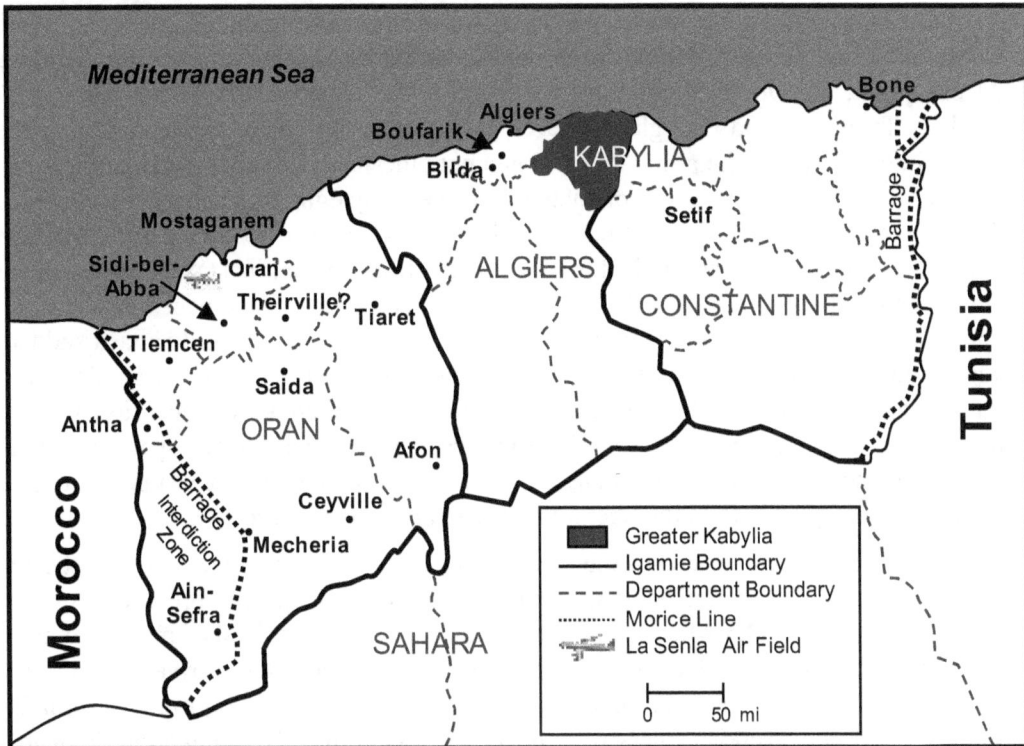

The cities comprised of only five to six percent of the population but exerted disproportionate influence over the country. The cities were the base moral, economic, and military power. They possessed the citadels, the seat of Shari'a courts, the *madrasas* and *kuttabs*, markets, trading posts, and access to the sea. The Turks dominated the political and economic life in the cities with the support of the janissaries. They balanced an exclusive caste system that promoted solidarity of the Turkish elite while at the same time allowed certain collaboration between favored local religious and tribal elites.[83] In the rural areas, the Ottoman approach to control emphasized the role of the tribe and sought to exploit competition between tribes to prevent powerful tribal confederations that existed prior to the days of Kahyr al-Din.[84] They accomplished this by giving certain tribes preferential treatment and by conducting campaigns against others to maintain their threats segmented.

The Ottoman political system consisted of three concentric circles. At the center is the city, the source of prosperity and power to which revenues and commerce flow. The first ring of the circle is composed of the *makhzan* tribes who benefitted from preferential treatment, often tax exemption, and constituted local militia. The next ring held the *rayat* who were taxpaying tribes (or villages). The final circle consisted of the dissidents who refused to submit or pay taxes.[85] Even within the rayat and makhazan there existed further divisions and forms of competition. For instance, one *makhzan* tribe may receive weapons and materials and not be required to collect taxes from the *rayat*, while another may be excused from fighting, and yet another is required to fight and receives no weaponry. Through these systems, they continuously checked the balance of power to keep their threats manageable.

The majority of the janissaries were garrisoned in or surrounding Algiers and rotated troops to a small number of *nubas* (outposts) scattered throughout important trade routes. At one point, the Ottomans attempted to control the Trans Saharan trade route as far south as Touggourt and Ouargla, however, this proved too costly to maintain and they soon withdrew back to the portal cities. When not otherwise actively campaigning against external threats, the janissaries conducted punitive campaigns (*mahallas*) twice a year.[86] These campaigns typically coincided with harvest and served to inflict punishment on belligerent tribes, test the strength of tribal confederations, and extract taxes. They typically employed auxiliary forces from the *mahkzan* tribes. A typical engagement was a raid, or a *ghaziya*. An aged practice in the region, in a *ghaziya* the expedition would attack suddenly against an unprepared village or herding camp and seize livestock, crops, goods, and on rare occasions women, while allowing victims to flee. On more severe occasion, the level of violence increased and at times whole villages and populations disappeared.[87] If the campaigns met with a serious challenge, they could withdraw and use sea power to mass reinforcements quickly to outnumber and out gun their adversaries.

During the end of the eighteenth century, the deys of Constantine and Oran became more and more effective at combining family politics and military presence to extend authority. In the east, Dey Muhammad ibn Uthman (1766-91) established military outposts in troublesome portions of Kabylia lands and deftly played internal rivalries to reduce significantly "the independent mountaineers' ability to spread sedition to the surrounding valleys."[88] Of note, Turkish rulers were never successful in fully subjugating the Kabyle people. In the west, Muhammad al-Kabir conquered the most powerful tribes between 1780 and 1797.

Ottoman power steadily declined throughout the eighteenth century under increasing pressure from European powers. At the same time the deys of Algiers were increasing the effectiveness of their beys and extending the government's authority, the sources of economic revenue were diminishing. European naval powers seriously decreased Ottoman privateering operations, and the colonization of Atlantic ports in Africa reduced the caravan routes of the Sahara. As the revenues diminished, so did the number of janissaries. By 1830, when France invaded Algiers, Turkish troops numbered only 3,700. In his book, *Modern Algeria*, John Ruedy describes a process of "deturkification" in the eighteenth century whereby "the state became increasingly dependent upon internal resources and hence upon the support of indigenous elites" and relied less on the Sublime Porte.[89] Economic and fiscal crisis peaked during the Napoleonic wars when a series of sanctions and naval blockades cut trade for almost eighteen years between Algiers and its traditional European trade partners. When trade finally resumed, much of Europe had found substitute markets and Algeria was unable to recoup its losses. Taxes levied on the *rayat* steadily increased as did the force used to extract them.

At the start of the nineteenth century, the Regency was in full-blown crisis. In 1805, religious elites mobilized the Oran province and parts of Titteri and succeeded taking Mascara and laying siege to Oran. That same year the ojaq in Algiers revolted against the Dey (Mustafa) and killed him, his treasurer and a prominent Jewish merchant who was responsible for securing commercial relationships with Europe. In the next eleven years, the ojaq and the divan installed six other Deys, and subsequently killed them when they were unable to satisfy all the factions and assure fiscal stability. Between 1810 and 1815, there were massive Kabyle revolts in the eastern regions fueled by religious elites in loosely associated with those in the western rebellion. In 1815, the United States declared war on Algeria, captured two of her ships with 200 corsairs, and forced the Algiers into turning over slaves and signing a treaty to stop privateering operations against the United States.[90] The following year a combined Dutch and British fleet British under Admiral Exmouth went to Algiers and forced the Dey to free slaves held as their possession. After doing the same to Tunis, he returned and demanded a treaty ending slavery and privateering. When the Dey refused, Exmouth bombarded Algiers for nine devastating hours firing 50,000 shots and consuming 118 tons of gunpowder.[91] The next day, Umar ben Mohammad Dey signed the treaty. A few months later, the ojaq assassinated him and nominated Ali Khodja to replace him. Ali Khodja proved to have keen survival instincts, made the bold move to secretly remover the state treasury from the Janina palace, and relocated his seat of power in the Qasba where he received protection from Kabyle and Kouloughli supporters.[92] With this protection, Ali Khodja Dey fought off an attempted revolt by the garrison in Algiers and repatriated or killed 1,700 janissary rebels. Ironically, he soon died from the plague. Before his death, he named his successor Hussein Dey, who ruled until the French made their entrance in 1830.[93]

In the twelve years that he ruled, Hussein Dey began to repair the Regency and made progress towards restoring control. Some historians offer that between 1817 and 1830 the office of the dey was beginning to takes steps towards becoming a true Monarchy by relying more on indigenous troops and by relaxing policies based on ethnicity to include Turkish descendants.[94] On April 29, 1827, Hussein Dey met with the French consul, Pierre Duval to discuss grievances of outstanding debts owed to Algiers by France. The Dey requested to know why the King of France had not responded to his inquiries, Duval responded that the King would not lower himself to correspond with him, and the Dey slapped the consul with a feather fly swatter. In June, a French squadron anchored at Algiers and demanded apologies and that the French Flag be flown over the Qasba in respect to the King. The Dey refused, and the French began a blockade, which it maintained until 1830.

The Ottomans were defeated by what they always feared the most, a European military power. They ruled a population of millions with a small and ethnically distinct military caste for the better part of three centuries. Their approach to control relied on managing the persistent conflict within their territories. The conflict among the tribes served to check the balance of power and ensure that no tribal confederation emerged to challenge the Janissaries.[95] This required constant maintenance in the form of punitive campaigns (*mahallas*) and raids (*ghaziyas*). They divided the territories into regions (Beyliks) and they too had to pay particular attention to the mountains of Kabylia. They established outposts in areas of that were strategically important to them (nubas) where they could control the flow of revenue and monitor the strength of the tribes.

On a few occasions, the Ottomans attempted to exert direct control of populations in the hinterlands, but the realities of the level of effort required outweighed the potential benefits and drew them back to the economic centers. They controlled the religious elite and scholars because they controlled the cities and the institutions that they offered. Through controlling the elite and managing the competition between tribes, they maintained enough power to protect their strategic interests and allowed local leaders enough autonomy to placate sentiments of social injustice stemming from their strict adherence to the ethnic caste system.

Islamist Movement 1988-2002

Since its independence in 1962, the FLN ruled Algeria as a single party system, and adopted many socialist policies based on substantial oil and natural gas revenues. The radical Islamist movement emerged as a major feature of Algerian politics in the mid 1970s. Under the neo-socialist, administration of Houari Boumediene, Algeria adopted a policy of Arabization. This policy set in place reforms to phase out the French language and replace French educators with Arabic speakers from Egypt, Lebanon, and Syria, many of whom were members of the Muslim Brotherhood.[96] In 1979, Chadli Benjadid assumed the presidency and began to slow down the pace of Arabization and socialist policies. Several factors led to this reversal strategy. Principally, a sharp decline in revenues from oil and gas meant that the state could not keep up with the demands of a rapidly growing population. The cities were becoming increasingly crowded with the young and unemployed, crime increased drastically, and health and housing services could not keep up with the demands. This resulted in a dramatic decline in the standard of living throughout the 1980s.[97] A number of religious and other dissident organizations began to emerge in secrecy since the regime did not allow other political organizations to exists.

In 1985, the Mouvement Islamique Algerien (MIA) staged protests against the single party regime (FLN) that included attacks on police stations and government offices. Escalating tensions precipitated by declining oil prices led to large-scale demonstration in October 1988. In September of the same year, the Islamic Salvation Front (FIS) emerged as one of the leading clandestine opposition organizations.[98] During this five-day event, more than 500 people perished in the streets of Algiers. The government of Chadli Bendjedid resisted temptations and calls to crack down on the demonstrations. The government continued to hope that it could either use the fundamentalist as a means to maintain order and absorb them into the FLN party system.[99] Following the riots, President Bendjedid put forth a referendum on the constitution to allow additional political parties to form. Numerous political parties emerged around ideologies ranging from labor unions, to feminist organizations, to Berberist, and finally to Islamic.[100] In September 1989, the government formally recognizes the FIS as a political party in Algeria. The FIS rapidly became the most popular Islamist party in Algeria with its base of support emanating from

116

large urban areas in Algiers, Oran, and Constantine. The FIS and other Islamic organization began to impose local rules banning, so-called, Western symbols of corruption such as alcohol and satellite TV and began to impose the wear of the *hijab* (veil) by women.

In June of 1990, Algeria held its first pluralistic municipal elections in history. In Algeria, municipalities carry considerable political weight due to the impact of everyday life and because they form the base of organizing national politics. The FIS achieved an overwhelming victory with 850 of 1500 municipal councils and 54 percent of the popular vote.[101] Through the remainder of that year and most of 1991 the FLN and FIS played a political battle of labor strikes and demonstrations (on the side of FIS) and electoral manipulation (on the part of FLN) which led to several postponements of the parliamentary elections. In June, Chadli Bendjedid declared martial law and had his foreign minister assume the head of state. The parliamentary elections finally took place on December 26, 1991 and resulted in the FIS winning 188 of 430 electoral districts. In fact, the FLN came in third place behind the FIS and the Kabylia based FFS of Hocine Ahmed.[102]

Faced with the possibility of a takeover of complete power by the Islamists, the Algerian military decided to intervene on the political process. In January 1992, the High Security Council (equivalent to the US Joint Chiefs of Staff) took over the government and installed a military junta called the High Council of State (HCE) to fill the constitutional void. The military coup leaders forced President Chadli Bendjedid and his Prime Minister to resign. In February, the military junta installed Mohamad Boudiaf, who had been in exile since 1965, as the seventh president of Algeria.

In March 1992, the government officially banned the FIS and arrested 5,000 former members. Subsequently several Islamist armed groups emerged and began to conduct violent campaigns against the government and the people of Algeria.[103] While the FIS remained a central player in the Islamist movement, a number of other groups emerged over the next three years to challenge the central government; among them were HAMAS, the Islamic Resistance Movement (MNI), the Islamic Movement Army (MIA), the Islamic Army Group (GIA), and the Islamic Salvation Army (AIS- militant arm of the FIS).

In June 1992, one of Mohamed Boudiaf's bodyguards assassinated the leader as he was conducting a televised address. The junta government reported that the bodyguard was a member of FIS sentenced him to prison. Noted historians on this conflict generally accepted that the FIS was not behind the killing and instead point to power plays within the FLN backed military junta.[104]   The HCE quickly named Ali Kafi as Boudiaf's successor.

Up until mid 1993, the Islamist groups (AIS, GIA, and MIA) targeted violence predominantly against government personnel (soldiers, police, and government officials) and against other Islamist organizations. Later that year Islamists killed seven foreigners throughout the country and announced they would kill all remaining foreigners after December 1. Some 4,000 foreigners headed the warning and left Algeria in November 1993. The GIA announced its intent to transform the Arab world into a caliphate based on the model of the successors of the Prophet.[105] After 1993, terrorism spread across all sectors of the population.

During this period the military Government took the opportunity presented by the violence to opportunity to rally political support for the regime from other parties, including the FLN and the FFS who were by now convinced that a democratic election of the FIS would have been a mistake. The government's initial main priorities in combating terrorism focused on cleansing the mosques of radical elites, protecting the infrastructure of the oil industry, and interdicting terrorist supplies of weapons and explosives.[106] Additionally, the government began to direct its Intelligence services to infiltrate FIS, GIA, and other organizations in order to draft in guerillas and exploit fractures between them. The government also conducted large-scale operations against known Islamist strongholds in the city slums and in targeted villages. Numerous reports from international agencies presented evidence of widespread torture and detentions.[107]

From the onset of unrest, the Algerian government showed a different approach to counterinsurgency than the one practiced by the French in 1954 even though they faced a very similar tactics. Instead of focusing on securing the population from violence, instead they focused on targeting the elites, protecting their strategic interests (oil and gas industry), and infiltrating the Islamist networks. The Islamist were first in taking the conflict to the population, but the government refused to play in a grand scale, and when it did it played by hard rules.[108]

Between 1992 and 1994, the attacks of the Islamists and the reprisals of the government and grass roots militias accounted for some 30,000 deaths throughout the country. An average number of forty to sixty persons were killed daily after May 1994.[109] The central government began to crack down on the press and by the end of 1994 controlled all press services in Algeria, and affected the expulsion of foreign press services. The international community could not help but take notice of the human rights violations and the obvious interventions in the political system. However, most economic powers did not want to see Algeria slip into an Islamic regime similar to Iran. In 1994, Algeria established a market economy and began large-scale privatization of former government run oil and gas industries. In doing so, they earned the seal of approval of the International Monetary Fund at a crucial time. That year it obtained 40 million francs from the international community in the form of loans, gifts, credits and other financial arrangements.[110]

Between 1995 and 1999 the Algerian government conducted counterinsurgency along three efforts; military/paramilitary operations focused on security, political reform, and control of the propaganda.[111] Conventional military security operations continued to focus on strategically significant areas pertaining to the hydrocarbon industry and in commercial and affluent sectors of the cities. Throughout 1995, civil authorities began to form village guards and other paramilitary units to provide self-defense to the population from the "*ghazias* of the Moudjahidin."[112] The central government distributed weapons and organized the militias using reserve soldiers, civic leaders, or tribal/family leaders. Some militias, established mainly in Kabylia, became active participants against Islamist organizations and worked with the army. The militias became a source of revenue and employment for many in Algeria and to some extent made the conflict profitable for the leaders on both sides of the conflict.[113] In areas where the Islamist was too strong, the army deliberately decided to abandon the population to the control of the Islamist. In a tactic which Luis Martinez, *The Algerian Civil War 1990-1998*, calls "Let-them-rot" the army isolated the areas (neighborhoods, villages) and allowed dissention to fester within.[114] In the border regions of the country, the army focused on interdiction of weapons and foreign fighters. The government enlisted the assistance of tribes and former rebel organizations in the border regions of Mali and Niger, which included joint patrols these organizations and the army. The border with Morocco remained tense and to this day proves to be difficult for the government to control.[115] In this manner, by the beginning of 1996, the government made major progress in exerting control over the territories and began to turn the tide on the Islamist insurgents.

Political reforms focused on transforming the military junta into a government that resembled a more pluralistic structure while reaching out to Islamist candidates with more moderate views. In 1995, the government established a, seemingly, formal division of labor between the newly appointed President, Liamine Zeroual and the military under the direction of the Defense Minister.[116] Later that year, the government held elections and Zeroual won the presidency in a semi-democratic process observed by international committees (Arab League, UN, and OAU) and declared free. Following his election, Zeroual passed a reconciliation law to allow former member of armed groups amnesty if they turned themselves over to security forces. The elections opened the door again for the government to re-establish foreign relations. In 1996, high-level US diplomats visited Algiers and signaled new levels of cooperation between the governments. Later that year, the US detained a prominent FIS member, Anwar Haddam, in Washington.[117]

The Algerian regime's approach to propaganda centered on tight control of the media and controlling the narrative that it produced towards Muslim and international audiences. In February 1996, the Interior Ministry revived censorship committees to allegedly control "security related matters deriving from non-official sources."[118] The government took every opportunity to deliver the message that it was protecting mosques from corruption, attacks, and politics. It delivered the message that it was protecting the right of all Muslims to worship freely and safely. In the international stage, particularly among western powers, the Algerian government delivered the message that it was preserving freedom and democratic principles from radical Islamic ideologies.[119]

Meanwhile Islamist organization continued to fracture and increasingly focused their attacks on each other. In 1998, the government began negotiations with a number of leaders of the FIS and AIS. Following the negotiations the government began released some historic members of the FIS. As a result, a number of Islamist groups conducted a series of massacres throughout the countryside to counter the reconciliation efforts. The practice of massacres against civilians caused serious splits in the GIA, and on September 1998, a new group emerged from former GIA members called the Salafist Group for Preaching and Combat (GSPC). As Martinez points out, by 1999, "the government succeeded in turning a conflict between Islamist guerilerillas and the security forces into a pitiless struggle between GIA and AIS."[120]

In 1999, former FLN fighter Abdelaziz Bouteflika, received the support of the army and won an arranged election becoming the tenth (and current) president of Algeria. Soon after his election, he concentrated on passing national reconciliation plan called the

Civilian Concord Law and increased negotiations with leaders of the AIS. In 2000, over 6,000 members of the AIS and other groups accepted reconciliation and returned to their homes.[121] The GIA continued to lose support, and many of its members moved into other countries. In 2002, the Algerian military killed the leader of the GIA, Antar Zouabri, and it effectively ceased to exist.

Luis Martinez likens the current state of Algeria, and the government's approach to control, to the Beyliks of the Ottoman Regency.[122] He uses the analogy to explain the nature of the conflict, the motivations behind it, and the approach of the Algerian regime. The analogy is particularly insightful when used to explain their approach to counterinsurgency. Faced with an internal threat, the military exploited conflict to consolidate its power and assimilate elites into the government. They focused their intelligence services on infiltrating insurgent organizations in an effort to manipulate their actions. Instead of focusing on the population, they focused on defeating the extremist elites, protecting their strategic interest, and managing conflict between militias and tribes. They used propaganda and draconian control of the media to control the narrative in the international stage and among other Muslim communities. In doing so, they exploited fears of Islamist movement to justify their actions, which included the morally offensive practices of the French counterinsurgency (torture, mass arrests, and suppression of free speech).

Conclusions

From their experiences in Indochina and in Algeria, the French developed a theory of counterinsurgency that focused on securing and controlling the population directly. The works of Roger Trinquier and David Galula propose that the key to winning the insurgency is winning the battle for the population. In essence, the population is the insurgent's center of gravity. Therefore, the counterinsurgent must drive a wedge between the insurgent and the population by establishing a level of security that is inhospitable to the insurgent's attempts to manipulate the population. Trinquier offers three principles that drive operations in counterinsurgencies, "to cut the guerrilla off from the population that sustains him; to render guerrilla zones untenable; and to coordinate these actions over a wide area and for long enough, so that these steps will yield the desired results."[123] This approach calls for a methodical and systematic campaign to secure the population and stop the violence, winning over their active support in a "strategic Hamlet," then spreading out from there to roll back the clandestine organization that supports the insurgent.[124] Their approach proved to be successful tactically in isolating the insurgents in areas that they controlled (within the National Boundaries), commensurate with the level of effort they exerted. However, the amount of effort required in terms of French troops (between 300-400,000 sustained between 1956 and 1960) and economy resources placed a heavy burden on the nation strategically as it tried to put decades of fighting and defeats behind. The preservation of a colonial state was a policy that drew international scorn from France's allies, and the tactics employed by the French (torture, mass detentions, and violation of international boundaries) further degraded their cause at home and on the global stage.

The Ottomans maintained power over Algeria for over three centuries with a small and ethnically distinct military oligarchy. They imposed a loose but effective system of control over the population by segmenting tribes and religious groups and promoting competition amongst them, while ensuring the balance of power remained on the side of the Turkish elite. The principle focus of the military was to protect their strategic interests emanating from commerce along the Mediterranean Coast and the Tran-Saharan trade routes. They established system of Beyliks and regions that provided them a means to exert control through elites. The elites were responsible for dealing with dissidence of tribal confederations. Thus, the warring parties unconsciously reinvented political organizations that supported the regime. Their tactics for dealing with direct threats consisted of adapting to the already existing practice of *ghazia* (raids) among competing tribes. When larger threats emerged, they conducted punitive campaigns that targeted not only the warriors, but also the entire population of the tribe/village. They exerted control over the religious and intellectual elites by controlling the institutions (mosques and schools) which supported them. As the base of their economy diminished, they instituted additional political reforms to incorporating indigenous elites into the regime to reduce the burden of maintaining a large professional military. This system proved effective at maintaining relative stability in Algeria; however, it degraded their ability to protect their interest from the European powers.

The Algerian military regime in 1992 adopted a modernized version of the Ottoman approach and defeated an insurgency in 2002. They initially focused their security efforts on protecting the regime and the hydrocarbon industry that provided the lifeline of the economy. Then, they infiltrated insurgent organization in order to promote fighting amongst them. As the insurgents stepped up and spread their attacks throughout the population, the military regime consolidated support from other political parties based on a common enemy. They armed tribes and local militias to provide self-defense in areas and to challenge directly the insurgents on their own strongholds in other areas. In areas where the insurgents were strong and strategic interests were not in danger, they adopted a "Let-them-rot" tactic that was the antithesis of population centric counterinsurgency.[125] On a number of occasions, the army reportedly allowed massacres and violence to worsen in certain areas, rationalizing that the population would eventually lash back at the insurgents on their own. They focused on co-opting, so called, moderate elites who were interested in the political process. They employed some of the same tactics of mass detentions, and torture that the French had in the 1950s, however, the international reaction was much less critical. Finally, the Algerian government strictly controlled the narrative of the conflict through a state controlled media to portray an image that they were fighting to preserve pluralism and the rights of all Muslims against the radical Islamist ideology.

The comparison of these case studies shows that both the Ottomans and the Algerians were more effective at combating internal threats than the French because they managed conflict within the limits of their means. The key difference in their approaches dealt with the tolerance of violence, the level of control required and the amount resources committed to securing the population. The French saw the population as the center of gravity, and population-centric counterinsurgency was a direct approach to that center of gravity. The French approach seeks to maintain a monopoly on violence and shelter the population from the insurgent's acts, or at least offer a better alternative for survival by collaborating with the counterinsurgent. David Galula offers that a key objective is "To isolate the population as much as possible, by physical means, from the guerilla."[126] This requires the commitment of massive resources to protect the population. The US Counterinsurgency manual recommends "between 20 to 25 counterinsurgents for every 1000 residents."[127] The larger amount of security forces increases the burden on society and increases the opportunity for discontent with security measures (checkpoints, searches, detentions, etc.). Security then becomes a right owed to the population by the government. The French approach sees violence as a risk and the goal is always to reduce it. Violence perpetrated against the population, by either belligerent, is a loss of legitimacy to the counterinsurgent.

In contrast, the Ottoman and Algerian approach viewed violence as both a risk and an opportunity. Their approach sought to control the population indirectly by relying on local elites. Both the Ottomans and the Algerians recognized that the means required for direct control of the violence were too costly and jeopardized the strategic interests. They each focused on securing strategic interests with the means available and embarked on the management of violence, as opposed to the control of violence. They accepted a higher tolerance for violence, and used violence coercively on the population. They made violence profitable to those who opposed the insurgent and focused on removing incentives for those who backed the insurgent. In essence, security became a commodity. The more invested the local population was in the central government the greater their chances at security. The Algerian military regime learned the importance of intelligence and propaganda from their experiences in the war of independence. They used this knowledge extensively to infiltrate the insurgent networks and manage the international perceptions of the conflict. This approach allowed the Algerians to localized conflict, exploited fractures within insurgent groups, and consolidated their power over time.

These case studies show that the French, Ottomans, and Algerians had similar objectives and effects they desired to achieve against the insurgents and on the population. The French employed a set of tactics that sought to directly influence the population in order to achieve greater collaboration and deny the support to the insurgent. After eight years, they were not successful in gaining the popular support to achieve victory and lost credibility at home and internationally. The Ottomans and Algerians employed an indirect approach consistent with their strategic interest that proved more effective at defending against internal threats.

This work did not set out to disprove the theory of population centric counterinsurgency, nor does it claim to do so in the end. In a process that historian John Lewis Gaddis calls particular generalization, this work set out to analyze how the counterinsurgency approaches in Algeria differed with respect to their outcomes.[128] Thought it shows that French were unsuccessful in achieving victory in Algeria with their model, it also shows that it was because the model was inconsistent with the realities they faced. In any campaign, a military commander assesses critical factors that define his strategic environment. These factors may typically include the threat, geography, economics, national values, history, beliefs, allies, technology, and national security interests. The commander then applies this reality through two lenses; the lens of the theory of action, and the lens of the collective aims and priorities of his nation. This analysis then allows for the creation of an operational approach. The only conclusion arrived at safely from this study is that, in Algeria, the

Ottoman and Algerian approaches were more consistent with their respective strategic realities. Obviously, the Ottomans approach to external defense was critically flawed. The French commanders allowed the tactical success of their approach to obscure their assessment of the environment.

The US counterinsurgency doctrine places a premium on lessons from the French experiences in counterinsurgency and the theories shown in David Galula's and Roger Trinquier's works. In essence, it has created an excellent operational approach based on assumed strategic realities, a theory of action (population centric counterinsurgency), and assumed aims and priorities. This study shows that, conceivably, the doctrine could use a more balanced perspective by analyzing approaches that have proven to be successful in other environments. The assumptions that drive the French model require the commitment of large amounts of resources over a long term and are well embedded in current US doctrine.[129] This leaves little strategic flexibility. The options are to either commit to a long and costly conflict, or do nothing. What this study shows is that other options exist historically that our doctrine should explore. While it may be intuitive to a rational thinker that a less direct approach to the population will be less effective or require more time, history in Algeria shows the opposite.

Notes

1.   Gian P. Gentile, "A Strategy of Tactics: Population-Centric COIN and the Army" *Parameters 39,* (Autumn 2009): 4

2.   Gian P. Gentile, 11.

3.   David Galula, *Counterinsurgency Warfare: Theory and Practice* (St.Petersburg, Florida: Hailer Publishing, 2005).

4.   Benjamin Stora, *Algeria 1830-2000: A Short History* (Ithaca, NY: Cornell University Press, 2001), 3-4.

5.   Luis Martinez, *The Algerian Civil War, 1990-1998*. Translated by Jonathan Derrick. The CERI Series in Comparative Politics and International Studies, (New York: Columbia University Press, 2000), 1-5.

6.   Martinez, *The Algerian Civil War*, 147. Messali Hadj had been released from prison and was under house arrest in Brazzaville

7.   A *colon* refers to a person of European heritage living in Algeria also referred to as *pied noir* by the French.

8.   Alistar Horne, *A Savage War of Peace: Algeria 1954-1962* (Middlesex, England: Penguin Books Ltd, 1977), 24.

9.   Alistar Horne, 25.

10.   Ratissage Operations entail isolating an area and then conducting deliberate search operations to flush out fighters, discover caches, and gain intelligence through interrogations.

11.   Horne, *A Savage War of Peace*, 27. The author also makes it a point to note the reputation of the Senegal units for their ferocity.

12.   John Ruedy, *Modern Algeria: Origins and Development of a Nation* (Indianapolis, Indiana. Indiana University Press, 1993), 149.

13.   Horne, *A Savage War of Peace,* 28. The Commander was General Duvall in a communiqué with the French administration.

14.   Ruedy, *Modern Algeria*, 150.

15.   Galula, *Counterinsurgency Warfare*, 64; Roger Trinquier. *Modern Warfare: A French View of Counterinsurgency*, Translated by Daniel Lee, Frederick A. Praeger, (London: Pall Mall Press, 1964). 8

16.   Trinquier, *Modern Warfare*, 65.

17.   Galula, *Counterinsurgency Warfare,* 74.

18.   Galula, 75.

19.   Galula, 78.

20.   Galula, 79-81.

21.   Horne, *A Savage War of Peace*, 83.

22.   Horne, 95.

23.   Horne, 98. In July 1954 French troops withdrew from Vietnam after being defeated at Dien Bien Phu. In June 1954, new French President Pierre Mendes came to power and

immediately instituted a withdrawal policy from Tunisia to lessen the violent backlashes occurring in the colonies.

24. Horne, 36. The term *pied noir* (black feet) is the name given to European colons in Algeria. By independence, the *Pieds-Noirs* accounted for 1,025,000 people, or roughly 10 percent of the total population.

25. For the purpose of this monograph, the works of Roger Trinquier and David Galula represent the French Theory of counterinsurgency. Understanding that there are other French officers who have contributed to this topic; the two authors are chosen due to their influence in contemporary US counterinsurgency doctrine and the existence of readily available English language works.

26. Roger Trinquier, *Modern Warfare: A French View of Counterinsurgency*, Translated by Daniel Lee, Frederick A. Praeger, (London: Pall Mall Press, 1964). 48

27. Roger Trinquier, 58.

28. Roger Trinquier, 28.

29. CRUA is derived from the French Acronym for *Commite revolutionnaire d'unite et d'action*. See John Ruedy, *Modern Algeria*, 155

30. Galula, *Pacification in Algeria,* 29.

31. Galula, 30-31.

32. Horne, *A Savage War of Peace*, 120-121.

33. Galula, *Counterinsurgency Warfare,* 58. Terrorism- While the term is contentious and there is considerable room for debate on the subject, this paper views terrorism as a means employed by a belligerent (non-state actor) to achieve desired effects against his enemy along a spectrum of conflict, typically used in conjunction with an insurgency. This definition is consistent with Joint Publication 3-24 *Counterinsurgency Operations,* which defines terrorism as "the calculated use of unlawful violence or threat of unlawful violence to inculcate fear; which is intended to coerce or to intimidate governments or societies in the pursuit of goals that are generally political, religious, or ideological," VIII-20.

34. Galula, 59.

35. Horne, *A Savage War of Peace*, 155.

36. Stora, *Algeria 1830-2000*, 46.

37. Stora, 48.

38. Galula, *Counterinsurgency Warfare,* 81.

39. Department of the Army, FM 3-24 *Counterinsurgency* (2006), 5-18. The term inkspot was coined by the British during their experiences in Malaya (1948-1960). The term and concept is closely related the French oilspot concept developed by Joseph-Simon Gallieni in the pacification of Indo China and later employed by the same in North Africa. See Douglas Porch, "Bugeaud, Gallieni,Lyatuey: The Development of French Colonial Warfare" in Peter Paret, Gordon Alexander Craig, and Felix Gilbert, *Makers of Modern Strategy: From Machiavelli to the Nuclear Age*, (Princeton, N.J.: Princeton University Press, 1986), 388.

40. Ruedy, *Modern Algeria*, 163.

41. Stora, *Algeria 1830-2000, 65.*

42. Ruedy, *Modern Algeria*, 165.

43. Matthew Connelly, "Rethinking the cold war and decolonization: The grand strategy of the Algerian war for independence," *International Journal of Middle East Studies* 33 (May 2001): 221-239.

44. Ruedy, *Modern Algeria*, 165.

45. Horne, *A Savage War of Peace*, 132.

46. Jean Larteguy, *The Centurions,*Translated by Xan Fielding, (London; Hutchinson & Co., 1962). The commanders of the French army of this period were a special caste of officers seasoned by years of fighting in WWII and Indo-China. These officers were the featured in the famous book by Jean Larteguy, *The Centurions*, and include famous officers such as Marcel Bigeard, Roger Trinquier, Maurice Challe, and Raoul Salan.

47. Horne, *A Savage War of Peace*, 166.

48. Horne, 160.

49. Horne, 187.

50. Horne, 188

51. Ruedy, *Modern Algeria*, 169. The CCE was constituted from the highest leaders in the FLN from the original members of the CRUA not already in French prisons. The members that were able to escape from Algiers were Abane, Krim (leader of the ALN), and Dahlab. These men took up refuge in Tunis, Tunisia.

52. Charles-Robert Ageron, *Modern Algeria: A History from 1830 to the Present* (Trenton, NJ: Africa World Press, 1964). 115

53. Thomas A. Bruscino Jr., *Out of Bounds: Transnational Sanctuary in Irregular Warfare* (Fort Leavenworth: Combat Studies Institute Press, 2006), 7. The Morice line was the most famous of the border fortification erected by the French during the war. It stretched over 200 miles along the Tunisian and 435 miles along the Moroccan borders and included electrified fences and state of the art sensors and cameras to alert the military of crossings or smuggling operations. At times, the French had as many as 80,000 troops deployed along the borders.

54. Galula, *Counterinsurgency Warfare*, 72.

55. Trinquier, *Modern Warfare*, 21.

56. Horne, *A Savage War of Peace*, 218. Saadi Yacef provided the location of Ali la Pointe to the French upon his capture. The French cordoned his hideout in the Casbah and set off demolitions charges when he refused to come out. The blast set off secondary detonations of cached explosives and caused the collapse of several adjacent building, killing seventeen and wounding four French soldiers.

57. Ruedy, *Modern Algeria*, 169.

58. Stora, *Algeria 1830-2000,* 51-52.

59. Horne, *A Savage War of Peace,* 238-240.

60. Horne, 266-267.

61. Horne, *A Savage War of Peace,* 247.

62. Trinquier, *Modern Warfare,* 102.

63. Ruedy, *Modern Algeria*, 172.

64. Horne, *A Savage War of Peace*, 281.

65. Horne, 309.

66. Stora, *Algeria 1830-2000,* 64-65.

67. Stora, 74.

68. Stora, 76.

69. Horne, *A Savage War of Peace*, 363-4.

70. Stora, *Algeria 1830-2000,* 80.

71. Horne, *A Savage War of Peace*, 441-3.

72. Horne, 458.

73. Stora, *Algeria 1830-2000,* 96.

74. Ageron, *Modern Algeria: A History from 1830 to the Present,* 126.

75. Tal Shuval, "The Ottoman Algerian Elite and Its Ideology," *International Journal of Middle East Studies* 32 (August 2000): 325.

76. Ruedy, *Modern Algeria,* 17.

77. The Janissary was Ottoman regular army. One of the first armies to be truly full time professional standing army.

78. Shuval, "The Ottoman Algerian Elite," 324. *Ojaq* is an Arabic and Ottoman term for hearth or fireplace. It originally designated a platoon-sized unit of men who ate, lived, and maneuvered together. It was subsequently applied to the whole body of Janissaries.

79. Shuval, 325.

80. *Taifa al rais* is the Arabic name given to the organization of privateering captains. Translates to the captains (rais) community (taifa). See Tal Shuval, "The Ottoman Algerian Elite and Its Ideology," 328.

81. Ruedy, *Modern Algeria,* 19.

82. Ruedy, *Modern Algeria*, 32-34.

83. Ruedy, 21-23.

84. Ruedy, 25.

85. Douglas Johnson, "Algeria: Some Problems of Modern History," *The Journal of African History* (1964): 224-225.

86. Ruedy, *Modern Algeria*, 35.

87. Thomas Rid, "Razzia: A Turning Point in Modern Strategy," *Terrorism and Political Violence* 21, (2009): 618.

88. Ruedy, *Modern Algeria*, 39.

89. Ruedy, 42.

90. Frederick Leiner, *The End of Barbary Terror* (New York, NY: Oxford University Press, 2006), 122.

91. Frederick Leiner, 178.

92. Kouloughli were offspring of Turkish fathers who received some preferential treatment, but were nonetheless excluded from holding official titles. See Shuval, 331.

93. Ruedy, *Modern Algeria*, 41.

94. Ruedy, 43.

95. Douglas Johnson, "Algeria: Some Problems of Modern History," *The Journal of African History 2* (1964): 223.

96. Hugh Roberts, *The Battlefield Algeria 1988-2002: Evidence and Analysis*, vol 2: (New York, NY: Cambridge University Press, 2000). 12

97. Martinez, *The Algerian Civil War*, xiii.

98. The acronym FIS is derived from the French *Front Islamique du Salut* meaning Islamic Salvation Front.

99. James Ciment. *Algeria: The Fundamentalist Challenge* (New York: Facts On File Inc, 1997), 154.

100. Martinez, *The Algerian Civil War,* xii.

101. Ciment, *Algeria*, 55.

102. Ruedy, *Modern Algeria*, 254.

103. Ciment, *Algeria*, 58.

104. Roberts, *The Battlefield Algeria,* 122; Martinez, *The Algerian Civil War,* 42, 133, 256.

105. Carlos Echeverria Jesus, "Radical Islam in the Mghreb." *Orbis* (Spring 2004): 1-13

106. Carlos Echeverria Jesus, 3.

107. Ciment, *Algeria,* 175.

108. Martinez, *The Algerian Civil War*, 226.

109. Stora, *Algeria 1830-2000,* 215.

110. Martinez, *The Algerian Civil War*, 228.

111. Echeverria, "Radical Islam in the Maghreb," 3.

112. Martinez, *The Algerian Civil War,* 152.

113. Martinez, 90.

114. Martinez, 150.

115. Echeverria, "Radical Islam in the Maghreb," 4.

116. The Military still appointed the President and the announcement of the division did not actually change who was in control but did allow a structure for politics to resume.

117. Echeverria, "Radical Islam in the Maghreb," 4.

118. Echeverria, 6.

119. Echeverria, 6.

120. Martinez, *The Algerian Civil War,* 19.

121. Echeverria, "Radical Islam in the Maghreb," 6.

122. Martinez, *The Algerian Civil War,* 220-244.

123. Trinquier, *Modern Warfare,* 65

124. Trinquier, *Modern Warfare*, 73; Galula. *Counterinsurgency Warfare,* 74-80.

125. Martinez, *The Algerian Civil War*, 150.

126. Galula, *Counterinsurgency Warfare,* 115.

127. FM 3-24 *Counterinsurgency* (2006). 1-13

128. John Lewis Gaddis, *The Landscape of History: How Historians Map the Past* (New York: Oxford University Press, 2002), 62-63.

129. FM 3-24 *Counterinsurgency* (2006). 1-24

Bibliography

Ageron, Charles-Robert, *Modern Algeria: A History from 1830 to the Present*. Trenton, NJ: Africa World Press, 1964.

Barnby, H. G., *The Prisoners of Algiers: An Account of the Forgotten American-Algerian War 1785-1797*. Oxford University Press, 1966.

Bruscino, Thomas A. Jr., *Out of Bounds: Transnational Sanctuary in Irregular Warfare*. Fort Leavenworth: Combat Studies Institute Press, 2006.

Ciment, James, *Algeria: The Fundamentalist Challenge*. New York: Facts On File Inc, 1997.

Clancy-Smith, Julia, *Rebel and Saint: Muslim Notables, Populist Protest, Colonial Encounters (Algeria and Tunisia, 1800-1904)*. Berkeley, California: University of California Press, 2007.

Connelly, Matthew, *A Diplomatic Revolution: Algeria's Fight for Independence and the Origins of the Post-Cold War Era*. New York, NY: Oxford University Press, 2002.

Connelly, Matthew, "Rethinking the Cold War and Decolonization: The Grand Strategy of the Algerian War for Independence" *International Journal of Middle East Studies 33* (May 2001): 221-245

Echeverria Jesus, Carlos. "Radical Islam in the Maghreb." *Orbis* (Spring 2004): 1-13

Gaddis, John Lewis, *The Landscape of History: How Historians Map the Past*. New York, NY: Oxford University Press, 2002.

Galula, David, *Counterinsurgency Warfare: Theory and Practice*. St.Petersburg, Florida: Hailer Publishing, 2005.

Galula, David, *Pacification in Algeria, 1956-1958*. Santa Monica, CA: Rand Corporation, 1963.

Horne, Alistair, *A Savage War of Peace; Algeria 1954-1962*. Middlesex, England: Penguin Books Ltd, 1977.

Johnson, Douglas "Algeria: Some Problems of Modern History", *The Journal of African History*, Vol 5, No 2, (1964): 221-242

Kaylyvas, Sathis N., *The Logic of Violence in Civil War*. New York, NY: Cambridge University Press, 2006.

Kaylyvas, Sathis N., "Wanton and Senseless? The Logic of Massacres in Algeria," *Rationality and Society 11* (1999): 243-285.

Larteguy, Jean, *The Centurions,* Translated by Xan Fielding. London: Hutchinson & Co., 1962.

Leiner, Frederick C., *The End of Barbary Terror: America's 1815 War Against the Pirates of North Africa*. New York, NY: Oxford University Press, 2006.

Martinez, Luis, *The Algerian Civil War, 1990-1998*. Translated by Jonathan Derrick. The CERI Series in Comparative Politics and International Studies. New York: Columbia University Press, 2000.

Michael, Willis, *The Islamist Challenge in Algeria: A Political History*. New York: New York University Press, 1998.

Paret, Peter, Alexander Craig, Gordon, and Gilbert, Felix, *Makers of Modern Strategy: From Machiavelli to the Nuclear Age*. Princeton, N.J.: Princeton University Press, 1986.

Pierre, Andrew J., Quandt, William B., *The Algerian Crisis: Policy Options for the West*. Washington, DC: Carnegie Endowment for International Peace, 1996.

Roberts, Hugh, *The Battlefield Algeria 1988-2002: Evidence and Analysis*, vol 2. New York, NY: Cambridge University Press, 2000.

Ruedy, John, *Modern Algeria; Origins and Development of a Nation*. Bloomington, Indiana. Indiana University Press, 1993.

Rid, Thomas, "Razzia: A Turning Point in Modern Strategy," *Terrorism and Political Violence 21,* (2009): 617 - 635.

Shuval, Tal, "The Ottoman Algerian Elite and Its Ideology," *International Journal of Middle East Studies 32*, (August 2000): 323-344.

Stora, Benjamin, *Algeria 1830-2000: A Short History*. Ithaca, NY: Cornell University Press, 2001.

Willis, Michael, *The Islamist Challenge in Algeria; A Political History*. New York, NY: New York University Press, 1997.

Trinquier, Roger, *Modern Warfare: A French View of Counterinsurgency*, Translated by Daniel Lee, Frederick A. Praeger. London: Pall Mall Press, 1964.

www.ingramcontent.com/pod-product-compliance
Lightning Source LLC
La Vergne TN
LVHW061259060426
835509LV00013B/1497

9 781780 398044